T0195889

LOWER ALABAMA BIGFOOT

No Longer a Myth

Ashley R. McPhaul

authorHOUSE®

AuthorHouse™
1663 Liberty Drive
Bloomington, IN 47403
www.authorhouse.com
Phone: 833-262-8899

Published by AuthorHouse   01/06/2022

ISBN: 978-1-6655-3986-9 (sc)
ISBN: 978-1-6655-3985-2 (hc)
ISBN: 978-1-6655-3993-7 (e)

Library of Congress Control Number: 2021920286

Print information available on the last page.

To my mom, who was a Bigfoot enthusiast before Bigfoot was cool. She told me tons of stories while I was growing up that scared me to death, but it was her stories that gave me the passion I have now.

CONTENTS

ACKNOWLEDGMENTS

First, I would like to give praise to Jesus, in whom all things are possible. Next, a huge thanks to my wife, who has supported and helped me with this book. To all of my children, even though they have been ridiculed for their dad believing in Bigfoot, stayed strong and didn't let it bother them. My kids are tough!

Also, thanks to Rocky Burch for your help with the maps and the cool story. Thanks to my cousin Adrienne for your huge help in translating and organizing my notes and thoughts. You are a hell of a writer, and I cannot wait to see your future books! Thank you to all my family for helping me and supporting me. I want to thank Wes as well; even though he is not a believer, he provided great support and helped me with this book.

Last but not least, thank you to all the witnesses who trusted me enough to tell me their stories. Without you, this book would not be possible.

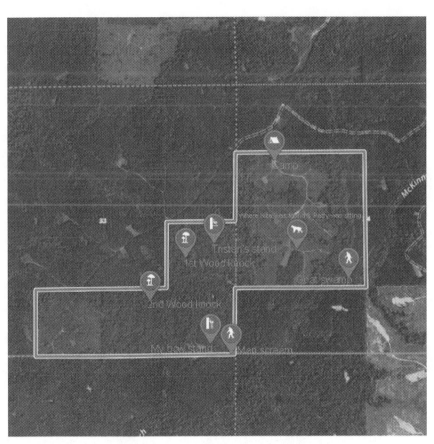

Map of Pine Orchard hunting lease

Sightings, Stories & Crossing Map

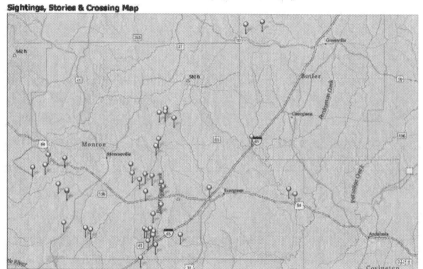

These pins indicate a rough estimate of the stories and sightings contained within

Map of the Bigfoot sightings in Monroe and Conecuh Counties

INTRODUCTION

THERE'S *SOMETHING* STRANGE GOING ON IN THE RURAL COUNTIES OF Lower Alabama. *Something* that makes hunters believe they need a bigger gun. *Something* that makes people nervous going into the swamps before daylight and coming out after dark. *Something* that has attacked animals and sent people running out of the woods. *Something* that's not normal. It defies logic, but it's happening and has been happening for years. People are finally starting to talk about it, and many of them are talking to me. It is my intention in this book to pass on some of the more interesting and credible stories to you.

I have been called a Bigfoot enthusiast, and I guess I am. But let me reassure you, there are no experts! And there never will be until we have a body or capture a live one. I am, however, about as close as you can come in these parts. There have been many books written on Bigfoot and many cheesy movies made. I've seen most of them, unfortunately, and read many of the books. This book is not meant to be an encyclopedia of Bigfoot facts or to retell every legend ever known about Bigfoot. What makes this book unique is that 90 percent of the events take place within thirty miles of each other. Several were within ten miles.

I should probably start by giving you a little rundown on myself. I left home in 1991 to go work for Uncle Sam during the middle of Desert Storm. I was a search and rescue corpsman with the marines. I missed out on spending time in the Middle East but got to see some great vacation areas firsthand on the continent of Africa, in Somalia and Rwanda. I flew on several missions in Somalia and was with some of the first boots on the ground in Rwanda. That could be a book on its own though, so I won't go into it here. I was proud to serve my country, as my father and ancestors before me had. Now, my oldest son, Tristan, is serving. God bless all the men and women, present, past, and future, who have served!

When I got out of the military, I went straight to nursing school, got married, and started a family (not necessarily in that order, if you know what I mean). I furthered my education and became a nurse anesthetist. I include this brief history only to let you know that I'm not totally off my rocker. Am I country? Yes. Crazy? Maybe. But, overall, I'm a pretty rational, thoughtful, and reasonable person.

Over the years, I have listened to many stories about Bigfoot, but I've included only the tales that I feel are legitimate. Like anyone from a small town, I know most of the people here personally, and I can assure you that they would never purposefully lie. I'm not saying that some may not be mistaken, but I can tell you that they know what they saw, and most had no clue that others had similar experiences in the same area. As you will see, the pieces of the puzzle kind of fit together. This is what has made me a believer and what I think will make you a believer too. Even if you're not a believer, I hope you'll find these stories as interesting as I have while doing my research.

Another important note is that some of the names may have been omitted or changed, but I've tried to keep the stories in the storytellers' own words as much as possible. I have also included a little bit of background on the rural communities around here where the sightings have taken place. Knowing some of the history and background will help bring the stories to life as we dig into this together.

CHAPTER 1
Where I Come From

I GREW UP AND STILL RESIDE IN MONROE AND CONECUH COUNTIES IN Lower Alabama. The counties are nestled darn near halfway between Montgomery and Mobile, about seventy-five to eighty miles from any major city. Growing up here, there was not a lot to do unless you liked to hunt or fish. Luckily, I love both. As a kid, I spent every minute I could either on my granddad's farm in Conecuh County or in the woods somewhere. The woods around here are very diverse. This area has pine trees, cedar trees, and a wide range of oak trees. Each brings its unique value to the terrain and animals that live here. These counties are rich with creeks, streams, rivers, and swamps. There are bottoms that are very deep, which most hunters can't get to. Due to the sparse population and variety in terrain, hunting here can be difficult. To me, it's not as much about the killing of the animal you are hunting as it is about finding peace and tranquility. There is no better air to fill your lungs than fresh pine mixed with earth. I do my best thinking and praying in the woods. I love the mystery and adventure of being in the wild. Eventually, I learned about everything that walks or crawls in these woods—or so I thought.

Monroe County is off the beaten path. You're not going to accidentally end up here. The population of the whole county is about twenty-one thousand. Our claim to fame is that we have been home to a few famous authors, two of whom are Miss Harper Lee, who authored the book *To Kill a Mockingbird*, and Truman Capote, who authored the book *In Cold Blood*. Once at Monroe County Hospital, I met Miss

1

Harper Lee and introduced myself as a nurse anesthetist. She thought somehow that I said I was a Baptist minister and told me real quick that she wasn't sick and was in no need of a Baptist minister! She was a very charming lady, and I got a good chuckle over that. Our industry here is primarily wood products and logging. We used to house Vanity Fair Mills textile factory and clothing outlet, but with the signing of NAFTA, Vanity Fair Mills moved to Mexico. The county has been struggling ever since.

Conecuh County, which neighbors Monroe County, has I-65 running right through it. The population is about thirteen thousand. Wood is again the main resource here, but the county is also home to the regionally famous Conecuh sausage. Both Monroe and Conecuh counties are rich in farmland, river basins, and swamps. There is something to hunt or fish here all year long. Not to mention, it's a short drive from here to some of the prettiest beaches in the world at Gulf Shores, Alabama.

My granddad was a tough leatherneck farmer with three hundred and sixty acres located on the county line between Monroe and Conecuh Counties in a small community called Bermuda. The farm was a beautiful place with lots of open pastures for cows and crops. There were ponds stocked with catfish and bass and plenty of woods, mostly filled with oaks. A crystal-clear stream ran through the middle of the woods. There was a lot to keep you entertained as a youngster. The town of Bermuda was nothing but woods and farmers, with three churches and a gas station. Today, there's not even a gas station. If you ever saw the television show *The Waltons*, my grandparents lived in a similar way. They had nine kids, with my mom being the oldest girl. I had uncles and aunts close to my age and even younger. With seven of those aunts and uncles still at home when I was growing up, their four-bedroom brick house was pretty crowded, but no one seemed to notice. As a child, the house seemed huge. It was nothing fancy, with each bedroom only big enough for a small closet and two beds. In the living room was an old Ashley woodburning heater, used in the winter to heat the house. I used to love the smell of burning wood mixed with the smells coming from my grandmother preparing dinner. In the summertime, the windows were open, and the fans were going full speed.

You may recall the 1980s began with a severe economic recession. For America's small farmers, this recession never ended. Farmers either "got big" or "got out." My grandfather was a fine farmer, but he was not cut out for the world of agribusiness. He eventually lost the beloved family farm, which changed all of our lives forever. Still, it was a great way to grow up. I remain very proud of the experience and the life lessons I learned. My grandfather is still the only man I ever met who could curse me in a loving way. It was his way of saying he loved me, and he loved picking on me. I do miss him!

In the evenings, my granddad would watch the news on the one TV in the house. Then it was time for *Hee Haw*. Right after the show ended, it was lights out and everybody to their rooms. After going to your room, you either read a book or listened to the stereo down low. Since there was no central heat or air, the windows were wide open on summer nights. You were able to listen to all the different sounds, such as crickets, cicadas, frogs, whip-poor-wills, and a variety of owls coming out of the woods. Aside from the insects, the nights were usually fairly quiet. We got the occasional chicken house bandit that would rouse my granddad out of bed. He would snatch his .410 shotgun off the wall and rush outside while mumbling a string of curse words.

My oldest uncle, Allen, was a former marine who served in Vietnam. He shared a room in the house with my uncle Wes, who was two years younger than I was. Wes was more like a brother to me than an uncle. Ever since we were able to walk, it seemed we were always in the woods. Allen was a master at hunting, fishing, and trapping. He taught me and Wes everything he knew.

It was fun learning to trap an animal or varmint, but we soon found out it could be a huge challenge, even though we had much more advanced brains. We had steel traps, live traps, and booby traps. Each was different, depending on the animal we were trapping. To trap a varmint, you have to understand a little bit about the varmint. You have to know his habits, what he eats, how he moves, and a little bit about what he's thinking. Nothing was more exciting than getting up at daylight and checking the trap lines that we had worked so hard to set the day before. You never knew what you would find. And it was always a great accomplishment to actually find what you were after in your trap.

If you do not understand the creatures you are trying to trap, then success is about as likely as winning the lottery. The odds are against you. I love to turkey hunt, and any good turkey hunter will tell you that if a turkey, with his keen eyesight, had the nose of a deer, a turkey would be a myth, just like Bigfoot! A turkey will frustrate you like no other animal. And it has a brain the size of a marble. How likely is it then that you are going to trap a creature that has the eye of a turkey and the nose of a deer, with a much more developed brain? Is this why Bigfoot is so elusive?

Stories of Bigfoot creatures go back generations, to the Creek and Choctaw Indians. The early Creeks and Choctaws, tribes that were native to Alabama, called Bigfoot the Kolowa and Honka. The names originally meant hairy, man-eating ogre but today translate to gorilla. Pretty accurate depictions!

There is a Creek legend of a warrior going off to hunt for several weeks across a river. When he returned, he found his canoe on the other side and had to swim back to the camp. Once there, he discovered his wife and several warriors eaten by the Kolowa. There is also a Choctaw myth where some brothers killed the one that ate their mother. There are well-known legends of Indian tribes out west that have very similar stories and depictions of these monsters.

I remember reading stories about them where they would sneak into the camp late at night and steal women and children. The warriors would hunt and battle them the next day but to little or no avail and at a heavy cost. They soon learned it was better to lose a woman or child every now and then than to lose your finest warriors. But I assume, as weapons technology improved, the scales tipped a little more in the warriors' favor, and the attacks stopped. Some of the reports I document in this book go back almost a hundred years in this area. There is no doubt that the early natives of this great state would have a few stories of their own as well!

Many of the stories I will tell you happened within just a few miles of my granddad's farm. To my knowledge, there was never an incident that actually happened on the farm. Wes and I stomped all over those grounds as kids. We would grab a blanket and sleep out in the open pastures or in the woods all the time. We were often scared but never saw anything like Bigfoot. My granddad, who was up with the sun, never talked about anything unusual. But the way my granddad was, even if he had seen anything unusual, he probably wouldn't have talked about it anyway. This is how a lot of country folks are and why some of these stories are hard to come by.

County Road 5, also known as the Federal Road or Old Stage Road

Langham Road

CHAPTER 2
Langham Road

THERE HAVE BEEN NUMEROUS Bigfoot sightings and a lot of activity near my granddad's farm. One such place is a dirt road called Langham Road. The connecting road is County Road 5, which borders Monroe and Conecuh Counties. County Road 5 is one of the oldest roads in Alabama. It split my granddad's farm in half. It is also called the Federal Road and is known in our area today as Old Stage Road. The Creek territory portion of the Federal Road was constructed in 1805 and ran from Fort Stoddert, Alabama to Fort Wilkinson, Georgia. It was a major travel corridor for American Indians, settlers, soldiers, and apparently other creatures. Langham Road, off of County Road 5, is approximately three to four miles long. And it is on this road where the Bigfoot obsession began for me.

In the 1980s, there were a couple of houses at the beginning of Langham Road and a couple at the end. The area in between was filled with thick forest and swamps. It was here where I learned how to hunt a new way—with dogs! A couple of Vietnam vets who worked with my dad at the hospital, Lavon and Doug, had the whole lease on this place. I don't know exactly how large it was, but it was at least several hundred acres. I don't remember any food plots or shooting houses at that time. We just "still hunted" with ladder stands and ran deer with dogs—blueticks, walkers, beagles, and black and tans!

Everybody who was somebody in hunting had some hounds. Nothing was more exciting to a kid than to hear those hounds strike up early in the morning, knocking the frost off the trees as they ran a deer toward you. Don't let anybody tell you that running dogs is not a sport! With a shotgun in your hand and the deer running ninety miles an hour, the deer would almost always win. Running dogs is a rare thing today. I find this tragic. These dogs were bred for hunting and running, and it was a thing of beauty to watch them work. The deer typically learned how the dogs worked as well, and nine times out of ten, the deer would outsmart the dog, especially back then, without all of the technological advancements we have today. Animals in general can be a lot smarter and more adaptive than people give them credit for. Keep that in mind as you read this book.

Hunting here wasn't so much about killing deer as it was an excuse to get out of the house on the weekends. The men got to miss church, drink all night, and tell stories. I felt grown, being allowed to take the occasional sips of beer or getting to drive the truck down the dirt road. My dad would go the few times Mom would let him, but usually I would load up the truck and head out with Lavon.

Deer down here were pretty scarce back then, nothing like they are today. Whitetail deer were introduced to this area back in the 1980s to help with repopulation—and repopulate they certainly have. We would ride Langham Road looking for deer tracks, and once we found some, we would set the dogs out, and the chase was on! There were times we would lose dogs. Some would just disappear and not come back. Some would come back with injuries that we would blame on a monster buck. Little did we know at the time ...

When I was older, my dad bought me a 1979 Scout International truck from Doug, and he gave me free reign to hunt the place as I pleased. Armed with a four-wheel drive and a huge place to hunt, I thought there was no stopping me! That is, until one fateful evening, I got it stuck. But let's go back to a few days before that.

I drove my Scout deep into a tract of land and parked at the mouth of an old logging road. From there, I walked a good piece, probably a half a mile or more, to an old cow pasture I had discovered on a previous hunt. It had long since been left abandoned. On the west side were planted pines. Toward the east, there were beautiful hardwoods. Separating the two was a wide fire lane that went down a hill. Now, I couldn't afford a rifle, so all I had was my dad's shotgun with three loads of double-aught buckshot. There wasn't any camouflage then either. It was blue jeans, long-sleeve shirt, jacket, and a pair of old tennis shoes.

I anticipated a deer would feed on acorns under the oak trees on the side of the pasture, walk down the fire lane, and stop to drink water at a little spring at the bottom of the hill. The plan was that I would be sitting there waiting to blast him away. I sat down under an oak tree, facing the pines and the stream. Hours later, it started to get dark, and a full moon rose above the trees. With the pretty moon, I decided to outlaw a little and sit for a bit after dark. In the state of Alabama, it is illegal to hunt at night, which is defined as thirty minutes before sunrise and thirty minutes after sunset. After I sat there a while, I was just contemplating getting up when I heard something up the hill, off the edge of the pasture. It was at the start of the fire lane, so I sat quietly, listening, with my gun ready.

I heard a loud snort followed by something large popping its teeth like it was aggravated. Now, at the time, there were only two animals that I knew that popped their teeth—a bear and a wild boar. Bears were almost unheard of down here, so I got excited, thinking I was about to kill a hog. I stayed still, and everything became eerily quiet. I was just about to the point of giving up, thinking the hog had moved along, when suddenly the woods erupted! Trees were snapping and popping, the ground was shaking, and something was coming straight toward me! It wasn't out in the open, coming down the clear fire lane, but barreling downhill from about ten yards inside the pines. The first thought I had was that it must be a bulldozer, but there was no engine sound. *What the hell is it?* As it crashed through the trees, my blood went cold, my hair stood up on end, and every instinct in my body told me that I was in serious danger.

Even though I had a shotgun with double-aught buckshot, my gut told me that it would just piss off whatever this might be. I looked behind me for a tree to climb up, but there was none close enough. I just froze. I told myself not to move, not even to breathe, and I didn't. I could feel its presence directly in front of me, but due to the thickness of the pines, I couldn't see anything. It was dark, and my heart felt like it was beating out of my chest. I sat there, lungs burning from lack of oxygen, for what seemed like an eternity, when suddenly another instinct kicked in and I started to run! I can remember a screech owl crying out overhead as I blazed the trail back to my Scout.

I fully expected to die that night, and when I got to the Scout, I expected to see the creature in my headlights when I cranked it up. In my mind, it had chased me the whole way back, but I'm not sure if it actually did. To this day, I haven't been as scared in the woods as I was that night. I went back the next day to look for prints or tracks, but a storm had come through late that night, and I found nothing.

What I didn't know at the time was that almost everyone who lived on this road or hunted here had a story or two. Many people I have talked to since have described incidents in the woods with very similar sounds, such as trees popping and the ground shaking. They even describe it as being like a bulldozer. Coincidence? I think not. These stories reassured me years later that I'm not totally crazy.

A week passed before I took the Scout on another adventure down Langham Road. I decided on a different spot this time and borrowed my buddy Moore's mini 14 rifle with a huge ammo clip. As I was hunting that evening, I felt spooked. The spot I had picked to hunt was off an old muddy logging road that went deep into some big pines mixed with hardwoods. I had a feeling that something was watching me, and I couldn't shake it. Not wanting to experience anything like I had the week before, I decided to leave well before dark. As I was driving out in the Scout, I got myself stuck in mud right on the edge of Langham Road.

This was before cell phones, so, frustrated, I hiked up the road about a mile to the closest house to get some help. It was a long and lonely walk, and eventually, I came up to an old farmhouse and knocked on the door. An older man came to the door, and I explained my dilemma to him. He had a four-wheel-drive truck and two tractors in his backyard, so I knew he could pull me out easily. He asked if I was in the hunting club, and I told him I was. He then got a little belligerent and told me that we had been killing his cows.

Now, let me tell you, everyone I hunted with was very experienced and knew the difference between a cow and a deer. They might drink and party every night, but hunting in the daytime was taken very seriously and was done very safely. Lavon and Doug would whip your butt in a heartbeat if you did anything stupid or unsafe. But I wasn't going to argue with this guy, so I told him I was sorry, and off again I went on foot. I backtracked the mile to where I got stuck and went another mile to a house at the other end of the road.

When I finally reached the house, near County Road 11, it was almost dark. There was a lady taking clothes in off the line, so I called out to her. I sure was surprised when she screamed and ran into the house. Now, keep in mind, this is a small community, and this isn't how people down south typically act. I was a little confused but continued on toward the house and knocked on the door. She opened the door, blushing, and apologized. I explained my situation, and she got a neighbor, Mr. Billy, to help me.

As I rode with Mr. Billy back to my Scout, he shook his head and said, "Son, I'm sorry for her reaction, but if you had been hearing what we have been hearing over here the past few weeks, you wouldn't be walking that road at night!" I asked him if there was a panther prowling around or something else. Mr. Billy laughed and said, "Son, I grew up here, and I have heard just about everything there is to hear. This ain't no panther." He described some of the hollers and screams and even made the point that, at times, it sounded like it was pushing over trees. Sound familiar? Mr. Billy said he and a friend went to check it out, but when they got close, it roared and sounded like it pushed down some trees, so they got out! He said it was very clear that their gun was not nearly big enough for whatever was out in those woods.

Mr. Billy also told me that at daybreak one morning, on his way to work, he looked out across his pasture, and on the edge of Burnt Corn Creek, there was something giant, walking on two legs like a man, at the edge of the trees. It was nothing like he had ever seen. I was amazed at what he was telling me. I decided to tell him about the man who ran me off his property earlier that evening. Mr. Billy quickly stopped me and said, "Boy, he's a grumpy ass all the time, but I've seen his cows. No man or gun killed those cows. Some of the yearlings had their head pulled clean off and were carried over the fence. He's crazy!" I felt a chill. My experience the week before was starting to make sense.

Mr. Billy's truck wasn't big enough to pull the Scout out, so we went back to his house, and I called a buddy of mine named Lee. His dad had a 1979 Ford Bronco, and he was tickled to sneak it over. He knew he would have bragging rights that his truck was better than the Scout if he pulled me out. We hooked up a chain, locked the Bronco in four-wheel drive, and smoked the tires down pulling. The Scout finally came out, but the Bronco was one big smoke ball! We just knew that we had torn something up, but to this day, I don't think his dad ever found out about it.

I ran into Mr. Billy a couple of years ago, and he told me another story. There had been an older couple living across the dirt road from him, and they had a hog pen in their backyard. "It was a full moon," he said, "and I heard an awful racket." He stepped out in time to watch as a creature was bending over and picking a hog up out of the pen in the backyard. He said that he was thinking to himself maybe it was some kind of a strange bear, but after the creature grabbed the hog, it slung it over its shoulders and walked across the road. The creature walked a short distance into the field in front of his house, and he could hear the hog squealing as it was being killed.

I have heard that there were several other incidents on this road in the years after my own took place. People just didn't talk about it back then. It is amazing to me how many of these reports share the same elements, even though none of these people ever knew of the other stories. A person who used to ride the school bus that went down Langham Road shared a disturbing memory with me not long ago. One morning, an elementary school–aged boy got on the bus with his clothes all ripped up. The boy had several scratches, and his shirt was torn like he had been in a fight. When the other children asked what happened, the boy said that as he was walking down his driveway, toward the bus stop, a large creature attacked him. The sun was barely up, so it was still a little dark. He had not been able to see exactly what it was, but he said it was bigger than any animal he had ever encountered. Luckily, before anything worse could happen, the school bus started rumbling down the road, and the creature took off.

Another witness who lived on the other end of Langham Road told me that back in the late 1970s or early 1980s, they found an oversized footprint behind the pump house one morning. This witness said it was about fourteen inches long and really wide. He remembers it very well because he actually called his brother over to look at it. During this same time frame, another resident claims to have been driving home from work when he saw a large, hairy creature run across the county road and across a field. The driver said he got a pretty good look at it and that it was definitely reddish brown and huge. This field just so happened to be one of my granddad's fields.

Another lady who lives on Langham Road said that one night her animals were acting crazy. When she went outside to check on them, she heard a loud sound, almost like a train coming through the woods. Whatever was down in the bottoms was screaming and hollering. She quickly went inside and locked the doors.

I met a man named Mr. Sam, a very well-known outdoorsman who moved to Langham Road in the late 1980s. He knew everything there was to know about horses and had several at his house. I heard a tale of him riding one of his horses through the woods when it started acting very strange. He said the horse almost threw him, and that's when he caught a glimpse of not one but two creatures. Mr. Sam said they were studying him and his horse. His horse didn't like that at all, and they were ready to get out of there in a hurry. Although Mr. Sam has now passed away, he became a believer that day and didn't mind telling anyone his story.

There was even a story of a couple of teenagers that I knew who would go parking on Langham Road occasionally. The way they tell it, under the moonlight, things were starting to heat up when suddenly they got a funny feeling that they were being watched. As if on cue, a huge, upright creature walked out of the trees and straight toward the car! The guy said that the car couldn't crank fast enough for them to get the hell out of there. Now I ask you, were all these stories made up? Has everybody just gone crazy? And if so, how in the world is it that they all happened in the same area?

Not too long ago, Lavon and I were burning some trash in the backyard. We had a pretty nice fire going and were drinking a few beers. We started talking about some of the old days of hunting and running dogs and eventually got on the subject of some of the weird stuff that happened on Langham Road. I told my stories again, and when I finished, Lavon just took a sip of beer and got really quiet. He finally said, "You know, I had a very similar experience many years ago and in that same area." You can bet I leaned in to hear the rest. "It was late, and I was still hunting, when all of a sudden all hell broke loose! Trees were being snapped, the ground was shaking, and something was hollering. It scared me so bad that I didn't even run; I crawled back to my truck! My gun felt useless." He said that until that night, he had never talked about it.

I wonder now how many other farmers and hunters have very similar stories but, because of fear of ridicule, are too afraid to tell them. When I asked Lavon exactly where he was in the area, wouldn't you know it, he was on the edge of the old cow pasture by the fire lane—the exact spot where I was hunting when I had my first encounter.

CHAPTER 3
Forest Home

As I have said before, I guess I'm a Bigfoot enthusiast. Never until my experiences on Langham Road did I ever think that these creatures could be down here in the South. When I was young, I remember reading some of my mom's books on Bigfoot. When my dad was stationed in California with the navy, she moved out there to marry him and started researching these monsters in her spare time. Her books fascinated me, especially all the pictures. But I always thought it was a creature that lived out in the western part of the United States and that it was probably dead or extinct by now. I also never imagined there might be more than one Bigfoot.

After nursing school, I started hunting with some friends of mine in a small, mostly forgotten town called Forest Home. Forest Home is located in Butler County, which neighbors Monroe County at its northeast corner. The last time I was there, the town consisted of one ramshackle country store and several old antebellum homes that had been long abandoned. The place we hunted was an old ranch that hadn't been farmed in years, with beautiful timber, open fields, creeks, and bottoms everywhere.

During this time, I had a certain buck pinpointed that I had seen back during turkey season. As soon as hunting season arrived, I had my tree climber, which is a device that a hunter uses to climb a tree and sit to watch and wait on game, set up in one of the creek bottoms. I was ready and waiting for my buck. I noticed wide trails were everywhere, but at the time, I thought they were deer trails. On one particular day,

I got up before first light and made my way into the bottom. I can remember distinctly as I walked into the bottom that the woods fell eerily silent. And I do mean everything just stopped. As I was walking down the trail, I got a very uneasy feeling that something was watching me. I thought I could hear footsteps walking with me, shadowing me. When I stopped, the footsteps stopped too. About that time, I heard a small branch snap, and I took off in a run! I ran all the way to my climber and scooted thirty feet up in a tree. It could have been a world record I was so quick. When I got settled, I remember laughing to myself, thinking I was going crazy and becoming a coward in my old age. Keep in mind, this is before everything that I know today. I actually killed that buck later on in the morning, and a few weeks after, I believe I found the answer as to why I was so stirred up that morning.

There was a guy who hunted with us from Mobile, who I will call Bob. I didn't know him very well, but he was a very serious hunter. He would go in the bottoms way before daylight each morning and come out way after dark in the evening. Bob had hunted pretty much every big game in North America and didn't mind telling you about it. Honestly, he wasn't overly friendly, and I really didn't care for him too much. But I will admit that he was an excellent hunter.

One morning, shortly before lunch, Bob came back to the camp early. His face was pale, and he blurted out, "You're gonna think I'm crazy, but I'm going to tell it anyway!" He told us that when he was driving out that day, he saw what he thought was a poacher walking the old barbwire fence line. The fence line was off an old cow pasture that had grown up in cedar trees. It ran into some hard timber and pines. He stopped his truck, grabbed his pistol, got out, and started walking toward the individual. Something seemed odd about him and just didn't quite feel right. As Bob got closer, he saw how hairy it was and realized this was no man. It actually appeared to be sniffing one of the fence posts as he approached.

"Now, I know what you're thinking, and you think this could have been a bear, but I'm telling you, it was no damn bear! This thing had shoulders and hands!" Bob said that about the time he got close enough, the creature turned around and looked at him. It stared for a second, got down on all fours, and hauled ass! Bob described the creature as having white circles around its eyes and being about six to seven feet tall. What unnerved him the most was that he had never seen anything that big move that fast. He said it went through a briar thicket that a rabbit couldn't have easily wiggled through, but this animal did it without any problem and with hardly any disturbance. He couldn't even tell where it went. Did it leap over it? Bob had been hunting his whole life and said he never would have thought such creatures existed. It changed his whole outlook as well as how he went into the woods from that day forward.

I could tell that Bob was in disbelief and almost angry about what he saw. He said that he would never feel safe hunting again. If you haven't guessed already, the briar thicket was just on the other side of the bottom where I killed my buck several mornings earlier, probably not two hundred yards away. Was this the reason I felt uneasy that morning? Did my instincts know something that I did not? I have learned through the years, especially as a hunter, you better trust your instincts. I believe this creature probably watched me go all the way to my tree climber. This was also the first time I heard that these creatures could run on all fours. As I would find out later, they definitely can!

Around 2003, I worked at a hospital near Forest Home in Butler County. I became friends with a lot of people who worked there and told some of them Bob's story regarding his encounter with the hairy man-creature. Usually, it was just to see if they would say anything or if they had any similar stories since they lived in the same town. Many of them did. There were several sightings of road crossings, morning and night, in the same area.

One hunter I talked with said that one evening as he was approaching his stand, his nose filled with an awful stench. Never in his life had he smelled something so horrible. As he slowly walked down the trail, toward some powerlines, he started feeling very uneasy. He finally popped out of the woods at the powerlines. There, ahead of him, probably a hundred yards, was a massive, hairy creature walking away. He said he quickly turned around, deciding it wasn't a good day to hunt, and left the woods!

Another very intriguing story came from a witness who talked to Lee Peacock, an editor with the *Evergreen* newspaper and a voice on the

Power Pig radio station. This witness was an elderly woman who lived in Forest Home at a very young age. Her school was just a one-room schoolhouse. She had a very clear memory that, at about lunchtime one day, a wild, hairy man came and looked in the window! The children and teachers screamed and huddled into the corner of the room until the creature decided to walk away.

As you can see, most all of the small communities around here have some kind of story. Just the stories in Forest Home stretch from about the 1930s to forties, to the early 2000s. Do these creatures haunt the same areas? Is there a healthy breeding population? It definitely seems that they do keep to some of the same haunts and trails. Hearing these reports got the wheels in my brain really moving—as hard as that may be at times!

Old store in Pine Orchard

CHAPTER 4
Pine Orchard

IN 2005, A FEW YEARS AFTER THE FOREST HOME ENCOUNTERS, I WAS fortunate enough to lease some land for hunting from a family friend. Little did I know there would be tons of Bigfoot activity in this place. It was about 240 acres nestled in a little town called Pine Orchard. This is just outside of Monroeville and Burnt Corn. Actually, probably twenty miles from Monroeville and about twenty-four miles from my home in Excel. Pine Orchard is another small community with a few old churches and one old country store. It was a thriving community in 1895 and, once again, is right on County Road 5 or the Federal Road. It's mostly in Monroe County, but it does extend to Conecuh County in parts. It's mostly just cattle farms and woods in this town today.

This lease hadn't really been hunted in years, and I was super excited to pick it up. Full of thick timber and small streams and creeks, this place was a deer paradise! I took my two oldest kids there one day to do some work and explore. Tristan, my son, and Morgan, my daughter, were probably twelve and nine, respectively. I was cleaning roads on the place while the kids were running and playing. I started feeling nervous for some reason. I did not want the kids out of my sight. The particular place at the hunting club that I was cleaning had an eerie, dark feeling to it. As a consequence, and to the kids' dismay, I kept calling them back close to me. I told them it was because of snakes, and, for the most part, it was. As anybody in Alabama will tell you, we have a rich variety of large, poisonous snakes, but I could not understand why I was so uneasy about them being far from me.

Later that hunting season, I was just letting Tristan start to hunt on his own. He became a skilled shot, was safe, and had shown good judgment. One weekend, Tristan, Lavon, Wes, and another close friend of mine, Tommy, and his son spent the entire weekend there to hunt with me. At night, we would build a fire, drink beer, and tell a few stories. We felt like we were living the life, and we were definitely making memories. I had long forgotten the uneasiness I felt on the club earlier that season.

One evening, Tommy let his son sit on one of the small food plots. These plots are smaller areas, usually half an acre to one acre, planted in a clearing and before the hunting season, with a variety of nutrients that are healthy for deer and that they love to eat. He was a year older than Tristan. Right before dark, the place erupted with, "Daddy! Daddy!" over and over. I heard Tommy yell from across the property, followed shortly by the sound of a truck cranking up as he drove down the road to get his son out. As we sat by the fire that evening, his son was almost hysterical, saying that he saw a black, hairy creature run across the back of the small food plot. *Whatever it was scared him pretty bad, but he's only thirteen*, I remember thinking.

Tristan looked up at me as we sat by the fire and said, "Dad, I want to hunt there tomorrow. Please? I ain't scared!"

So, laughing, I said, "Sure, we can make that happen." Tristan, after all, had something to prove: he was a bigger man!

The next evening, I hung my climber close to him and put him in the same shooting house as Tommy's boy had been in the day before. A shooting house is an enclosed structure, built off the ground, near a food plot, where a hunter can sit in, safe from the elements, and watch for deer. I left the four-wheeler outside the patch, at the end of the lane, to make Tristan feel better. I headed to my own spot, eased up in my climber, and waited. Close to dark, I could hear some deer starting to move toward me. I was just getting my gun ready when suddenly I heard "Daddy, Daddy, Daddy!" It was Tristan! Cursing to myself, I got down and started moving quickly toward where he was.

A few minutes later, Tommy showed up with Tristan. I was really mad and, honestly, was about ready to snatch him up. One look at him, though, and the anger quickly went to concern. He was one scared twelve-year-old boy and was literally shaking. I asked him what had happened. He said he was in the shooting house when he heard something come up behind him. There was a funny noise, like bones crunching. I figured this was how a twelve-year-old would describe something popping its teeth. He got his gun ready when suddenly something grabbed the shooting house and started shaking it. "My body just told me to run, so I did!" He said it almost shook him out of his chair.

Tristan said the shooting house was moving pretty good. He ran so fast that he left the four-wheeler on the road and went a good distance to the next food plot where Tommy was sitting. The whole time, he was yelling for me. As Tristan ran out of the shooting house, he looked back at it as it came across his left side. He was terrified to see there was a tall, black, hairy creature, taller than the shooting house roof, trying to shake it and look inside.

Now, this shooting house was made out of trampoline bars, and the roof stood approximately six to seven feet off the ground. It was pretty solidly built with a wide base. As Tristan ran, he heard some crashing. He thought it was coming after him and figured he did not have time for the four-wheeler. I found evidence later that that creature was going the opposite way, toward a creek branch. As I looked around on the road that it ran down, I noticed what looked like footprints. I actually have Polaroid copies of these pictures, which are included at the end of this chapter. You could clearly see eleven- to twelve-inch footprints in a straight line with toes. I did some research later, making sure it wasn't a black bear; there is no black bear on record with a footprint this big. Not to mention, they were in a straight line, which I found odd.

When I found those footprints, the anger set in. I got pissed off and ran toward the creek branch, where I figured this creature had gone. All up along the creek branch, I found limbs snapped off seven to eight feet off the ground where it ran down the creek. It gave me the impression that this creature was as mad as I was. There was no other explanation for the snapped limbs. I tried to convince myself that it was a bear, but my gut told me deep down that it wasn't. Wes was with me, and he couldn't make sense of it either.

A couple of weeks later, I was hunting in the same area on a wooden ladder stand. I was just about asleep when I heard a loud cracking sound. Now, this was late in the evening, and it was getting dark. The crack sounded like a limb popping loose from a giant tree, but I never heard the thud you'd expect from it hitting the ground. This noise startled me so much that I nearly fell out of my stand. It was only about fifty yards behind me. Suddenly, I heard another crack answer it! This was farther, probably 150 yards down to my left, off the property line. It was even darker now, and to get out, I had to walk right past where the first crack sounded off. Once again, my hair started standing up as I was sneaking down the tree. Apparently, this sound is called a "wood knock," a term that Bigfoot researchers use. They believe that this knock helps a Bigfoot locate other Bigfoot in the area and serves as a warning of potential danger. I had no clue at that time what it was. The only thing I knew was that it seemed weird and that it did not happen naturally. This, again, was very close to where Tristan had his scare.

Everyone who has hunted here has had some kind of experience or another. But, of course, not everyone talked about it until much later. I just found out a few months ago that Tommy had been hunting on a food plot in Pine Orchard one evening, and he heard something so horrific, hollering down in the bottom, that he walked back to his truck and sat there till dark. He came back to the camp, told everybody he did not see anything, and chose not to tell anyone that he had been sitting in his truck. He decided that he was not going to be the brunt of the jokes that evening around the campfire.

One of my mother's younger sisters, Patty, and her brother, Wes, decided to hunt up in Pine Orchard one weekend. This was on the other side of the property, on a large food plot. Off to the side of the food plot, down a little road, was what we call Goat Swamp. This little swamp runs kind of behind where Tristan was sitting on the other side of the property. Patty got up before daylight and headed to the shooting house, which, at the time, we had on the ground. As she was walking to get in the shooting house, she looked down Goat Swamp Road, and something huge and upright was moving out of the swamp, onto the road, ambling toward the shooting house.

A little panicky and not sure what it was, being that it was still dark, Patty quickly got in the shooting house and sat down. A few seconds later, she said something walked within ten feet of her. She had to duck down and look up out of the window to see the creature as it quietly walked past the shooting house into the plot. She said it was at least as tall as a horse. It never stopped and never looked at her or even seemed to care that she was there. It just walked through the plot and headed down in the bottom, exactly where Tristan's food plot was. Laughingly, today, she says she almost peed her britches and that she would not leave the shooting house until Wes came and got her later that morning.

Months would go by, and things would seem normal. I would dismiss all the stuff that happened before, and then, out of nowhere, it would start again! I have observed, at least down here in Lower Alabama, that you can usually tell the creature is around by the coyotes. The coyotes always seem to be right on its heels. I would hear a howl, and then suddenly the coyotes would go nuts, constantly barking and howling. Maybe they were looking for scraps and had learned to follow those things for food. There were several nights that I stayed in Pine Orchard by myself in our little camper. Sometimes, I swore I heard footsteps outside the camper, while coyotes were howling in the distance. One thing is for sure: if you are hunting in Lower Alabama and start hearing the coyotes going nuts, you better be aware.

One spring around 2008, Tommy's nephew begged me to let him go turkey hunting up on this 240 acres that I leased in Pine Orchard. He had no idea of any of the things that had happened up here. I agreed and even let him borrow my Bronco since he did not have a four-wheel drive. I had to sell my Scout years before when I went into the military. The transmission had gone out, and I didn't have enough money to fix it. I was brokenhearted and ended up selling it for $300. The guy who bought it still has it to this day. I only mention it because he told me that I might get an opportunity to buy it back one day, so I'm sending him a copy of this book!

Anyway, Tommy's nephew headed off to Pine Orchard and the next morning called me all in a panic, asking if I had played a joke on him the previous night. Never having disclosed any of the prior experiences encountered in Pine Orchard to him, I told him no. I was on call for the hospital that night and therefore could not have been that far away. Not to mention the fact that I was not going to drive twenty-two miles in the middle of the night to play a joke! I asked him what happened. He said he had cooked on the grill that night and finally eased himself into the bed about nine o'clock. Sometime after midnight, he was awakened by something walking outside the camper. It sounded like it was messing with some of the leftover food that he had cooked on the grill. He had decided it was probably a possum or a raccoon and dozed off again. The nephew was jolted awake by a scream. He said, "Ashley, it sounded like a man scream, not a panther. It was deep and loud!" He described it as being so close to the camper that the camper was literally vibrating when it sounded off. It did not scream once but screamed three times. His heart felt like it was going to pound out of his chest, and he said it was like nothing he had ever heard in this world.

Unfortunately, he left his shotgun in the Bronco, which was probably ten to fifteen feet outside the camper. He was too scared to go outside and get it, so he stayed up all night. He never moved, for fear that it would hear him inside the camper. When the sun came up, he decided it was time to get out. I didn't really understand what he heard until later, but I ran into him about a year ago, and he still tells the same story. Even repeating it, you can see the hairs starting to stand up on his arms! He has not been back to hunt there since that night.

Every year, I have a couple of buddies from Mississippi, Tom and Eddie, come over and hunt during the rut. They have been making this annual trip for years, and they know the lore of the place, but nothing has ever happened to either one of them. One evening, though, just this past year, Tom and I heard a pretty distinct howl near Goat Swamp, moving through the bottom. It howled several times and literally made Tom stop on the four-wheeler. He came out, wide-eyed, asking me, "What was that?"

I just laughed and said, "You know what it probably was," and we just moved down toward the camp.

That evening, the three of us caught up over the campfire while drinking plenty of beer, as friends tend to do. Eddie swore to Tom and me that he may have heard a wood knock that day. Later that night, we turned in and fell into a deep sleep. The next morning, Eddie started asking us if we remembered the camper being shaken during the night. Tom and I laughed and told him that he was probably just dreaming. He shook his head and swore that it jarred the camper so badly that it made him sit straight up in the bed.

I didn't think much of it at the time until my youngest son, Ashton, and I were turkey hunting the next spring. We decided to try to roost a turkey that evening, staying overnight to see if we could close the deal the next morning. About one in the morning, I was awakened up by a massive jarring of the camper. The camper damn near felt like it was going to come off the ground. It was as if a truck or a giant limb had hit it. Ashton was still sleeping and just rolled over. I grabbed my gun and my light and went outside. Nothing. Morning came, so as soon as it became light outside, I checked the trailer for a dent or for a large limb and still found nothing. I didn't make fun of Eddie anymore after that night.

The next deer season, I shot a nice buck in the neck in Goat Swamp. There was blood everywhere, and I knew there was no way he could be more than fifty yards away. I waited an hour, went in there, and found nothing. The blood trail just stopped. Very few deer have ever walked off from my 308, but this one did, and it is still a mystery to me today. I searched for that buck for two months afterward, with not a trace. Just to emphasize how unusual this is, I will tell you that Ashton made a good shot on his first buck, but I accidentally pushed him too soon. The buck got up and ran three hundred yards without hardly a drop of blood. I found it about three days later just by watching the buzzards.

I decided at this point that I needed a dog. A blood-trailing dog! Not to mention the fact that it would probably make me feel just a little safer being up there all night by myself. So, after doing some research, I came up with the perfect dog. A Catahoula. These dogs were born to hunt. They have adapted to the swamps and go back to the Choctaw Indians for deer and hog trailing. The French perfected them with strict lining, a type of breeding, over the next one hundred years. A regular hound usually won't do. That's not what they are bred for. Hounds will chase the freshest deer scent. If it's the blood, you're in luck, but if it's a doe that runs across the blood, then those dogs will go another mile or so, chasing the doe into another county.

So, off to Louisiana I went to get myself a Catahoula! I named her Nita, and she was my baby, even sleeping with me for the first couple of months. She was just getting tuned in to finding wounded deer, with one successful mission already. I took her every time I went out, hoping we could get some blood on the ground. She was still very young and would never go far from where I was. At times, she would sit in the shooting house with me or Ashton. Even though we wouldn't see a deer, she would growl low and let us know that one was about to come out on the food plot. This dog was pretty amazing.

The next bow season, I loaded up Nita, and we headed to Pine Orchard to do an evening hunt. I love bow hunting and couldn't wait to get out there. I locked Nita up inside the camp house, and off I went to go hunt under some white oak trees that were dropping acorns. I remember the date exactly. It was November 8, 2016. I can remember being high up in an oak tree in my climber while keeping tabs on the election on my phone, wondering if President Trump was going to pull it off. It was just getting dark when I heard a howl down toward Goat Swamp.

Quickly, as usual, the coyotes cut it off. For a few minutes, I sat there listening, but all I could hear were the coyotes. It was getting too dark now to shoot my bow, so I decided it was time to get down. I eased my arrow into my quick quiver and tied my bow on my string. I was just starting to drop it to the ground when suddenly, out of nowhere, there was a huge scream! At first, I thought it was a man yelling for help. What started out deep in tone quickly crescendoed into a high-pitched scream. It was immediately clear to me that this was the man scream that Tommy's nephew had heard. There could be no mistaking it.

Usually, because of all the activity up there, I carry a pistol with me. But not that day. It was just a quick hunt, and I didn't even have a flashlight. This scream blasted me and stopped me dead on my climber. I actually considered going back up higher in the tree. The howl was probably two hundred yards away from me, but I could actually feel it vibrating on my chest. The only way to describe it is that it sounded like a cross between an eight-hundred-pound man and a firetruck. There is absolutely nothing in those woods that could make that kind of sound!

I knew exactly what it was. I could not have been more convinced if one had come up and slapped me. After a few minutes of sitting, stunned, I knew that I had to get out of there. The howl, or scream, was in the opposite direction of my truck. Before I snuck down from the tree, I can remember distinctly praying, "Lord, I have always wanted to see this thing, to know for a fact that it's real, but not tonight. Especially with a bow in my hand!" I made it back to the truck, constantly looking over my shoulder as I was walking out through the hardwood bottom. It seemed like there wasn't a sound anywhere in the woods now. Then, as if on cue, the coyotes started back up and went crazy! They sounded as if they were almost on the very spot where the scream occurred. I went back to the camp, grabbed Nita, and we left. I can remember how grateful I was to see my truck and my dog. Whatever that thing was, I knew without a doubt that with him in the woods, he was the boss!

I went back the next morning to hunt again, this time in a different area. The coyotes were still hollering in the spot from the day before. I did at least have my pistol on me this time. I didn't know what the scream from the day before meant. I don't know if it knew I was there. Why were the coyotes still in the same area, hollering? I honestly think the creature was hunting in the swamp that evening. The scream stunned its prey long enough for it to kill it, and the coyotes were still eating the leftovers. It is the only explanation I can come up with. But as long as I live, I will never forget what I heard that evening. And I now know exactly what Tommy's nephew must've gone through, hearing it that close to the camper not once but three times!

A few weeks later, gun season came in, and off to my lease I went, with Nita riding shotgun beside me. We went into Goat Swamp, looking for signs of a buck. We found a few, so I hung my climber. Nita and I stopped at the big food plot on top of the hill, where my aunt Patty had her experience. The wind was blowing fiercely that day. I knew I was wasting my time, but sometimes you just have to go when you're off work, regardless.

Nita saw something and took off on the side of the plot. I didn't worry much because I had a bell on her, and she never went very far. After a few minutes, I called to her but got no response. I couldn't hear her bell because of the wind, so I honked the horn. I went a couple hundred yards down the road, looking at another spot, went back to the plot, and still nothing. Now I was getting a little worried and a little aggravated. Maybe she jumped a deer and decided to run it and was on the other side of the property.

I drove my truck to the other side, looking for tracks, and didn't find anything. I drove back to the plot one last time, yelled, and blew the horn but still didn't see her. Nor did I hear her. I decided that I would go back to the camp, change clothes, and hunt. I thought I would park the truck on the plot. That way, if Nita came back, she would see the truck and load up. By the time I reached the camp, changed, and headed back out to hunt, about forty-five minutes had passed since I had last seen Nita. This was not typical behavior for her.

I was heading back to the plot to park my truck when I spotted my dog. She was lying on her side in the road that leads into Goat Swamp and wasn't moving. I couldn't believe it. I walked up to her, staring in disbelief. I knew she was dead. Did I accidentally run over her? I checked her fully, and there wasn't a mark on her. No broken ribs, no blood anywhere. It was a little warm that day, so I checked for snake bite marks. With tears in my eyes, I picked her up and put her gently on the back of my truck. The first thing I noticed was that she was already stiff, except for her head and neck, which were floppy.

Did she have a broken neck? I called the local vet, and he couldn't make sense of it either. She was young and in good shape, he said. He offered to do an autopsy, but I decided against it. He said that only massive trauma or a heart attack would cause her to be that stiff that quickly. And there was a possibility of a broken neck. "She could've even been scared to death," he said. I guess I will never know because I buried her up there that evening. Then, gritting my teeth in anger, I grabbed my rifle and went and hunted on my stand in Goat Swamp.

I prayed that I would see whatever it was that may have hurt my dog. I followed Nita's tracks into the swamp. She went back in there looking for me when I was off the plot. I only found one track coming out of the swamp, but not the first track going back to where her body lay. If it was this monster, did it put her in the middle of the road for me to find? Was it trying to tell me something? I don't know, but I knew if it showed its face that evening, there was going to be payback for sure. I miss that dog to this day, and her sudden death still remains a mystery. Or maybe it's not so much of a mystery anymore. What I didn't know then is that this was not the end of the story for Pine Orchard.

My camp in Pine Orchard

My camp in Pine Orchard

Goat Swamp Road—where Patty was sitting and where Nita was found

Beginning of Goat Swamp

Tree snapped in Goat Swamp

Watery foot impressions in Goat Swamp

A structure in Goat Swamp

Old Polaroid picture from 2006–2007
Closeup of footprints near Tristan's stand after the shooting house was shaken

Old Polaroid picture from 2006–2007
Footprints near Tristan's stand after the shooting house was shaken

CHAPTER 5
What Do We Know

As mentioned earlier, I have read many books and watched countless movies on this subject. When I was young, before I could even read, I would look at some of my mom's Bigfoot books and stare in amazement at the pictures of the tracks, the creature and proposed evidence. There are many theories on this creature, from being an alien, to interdimensional, to being a missing link or even a descendant of Gigantopithecus. "In the folklore of many Native American tribes, as well as the indigenous people of the Himalayas, the animal is said to be a peaceful, supernatural creature with intelligence and spiritual powers" (Harris 2021). In the movies and books, he ranges from everything from a bloodthirsty killer to a family-friendly animal activist. But one thing for sure is most places in the world have had and still have stories of this creature that have been passed down for centuries.

What do we know for sure? What can we say for a fact that we can't deny? I feel that these are some of the questions we must start with. Hopefully by now you have seen several similarities in the accounts here in Lower Alabama. You will find more as you continue to read. We know that these folks in this close proximity are seeing something. I don't believe that every story is made up or a case of mistaken identity. The facts are hard to ignore here. The only creature in this part of the country that could come close to pulling off a case of mistaken identity is a black bear.

Black bears are large and can vary in size depending on their environment. According to Kaiya McGhaw (2019), "males typically average between 150 to 300 pounds with the largest male recorded thus far at over 900 pounds." The paw size of a bear is directly linked to the bear's weight. Jae Allen (2018) explains that black bears with "a front paw print of 5 inches long is average, equating to an average weight between 150 and 175 pounds." Simply put, the bigger the paw print, the bigger the bear. Allen (2018) continues, "a 7inch paw print is from a bear weighing 300 to 400 pounds." These paw sizes are much smaller than the tracks I found in Pine Orchard after my son's experience. This is also smaller than the tracks found by others in this area.

Bears do tend to "snarl, show their teeth, pop their teeth together for sound, and salivate heavily" (Toole). This same type of behavior has been reported with many eyewitness accounts. However, a bear cannot run on two legs, nor do they have shoulders—two characteristics that most all eyewitness accounts include. Once abundant in black bears, we see that our "black bear populations in Alabama have been almost completely depleted and are now threatened with local extension due to their small population size, fluctuating sources of food, and human caused death" (McGhaw 2019). Even though it appears Alabama's black bear population is diminishing, McGhaw (2019) explains that "overall black bear numbers have increased in recent years throughout North America and the American black bear is listed as an animal of least concern by the International Union for the Conservation of Nature Red List of Threatened Species."

What else do we know? Although there are sightings all over the South, it seems unusual to have so many in this close proximity. Lyle Blackburn (2017) wrote a book called *Beyond Boggy Creek*. He investigated numerous similar sightings all over the South, from Texas to North Carolina. The stories again are very similar in nature. The eyewitness reports describe the creature in the same way, such as huge, broad chested, with a color ranging from red to black and brown, and anywhere from six to ten feet tall.

Another thing that seems to be true and was explored in the film *The Legend of Boggy Creek* (1972) is that these creatures always follow the creeks. Most sightings around here seem to follow that pattern, and in this area, as you can see with our map on page xii, it's Burnt Corn Creek. There are tons of other water sources here, including the

Alabama River and a plethora of other swamps and creeks, but that particular creek appears to be a major travel area. What made that 1972 horror film unique is that all the sightings and encounters were in close proximity. It literally turned that town upside down. So, can all these stories around the South, much less the stories in this book, just be coincidence? I will let you decide.

So, what are we left with? We are left with the fact that all these accounts—my own accounts and others—are either fabricated, cases of mistaken identity, or hallucinations. Or we are left with the conclusion that something else is out there. Something that, even with eyewitness reports, tracks, and hair samples, science for the most part refuses to acknowledge. Why? Because we don't have a body. Fossils have not been uncovered, but this may be due to several factors. Harris (2021) explains that "it is quite likely that the bones would go undiscovered, since there has been a full-blown, scientific search for them." Everyone has an opinion about what these encounters might be. One possibility is that maybe this creature is a descendant of Gigantopithecus. Did Gigantopithecus really exist? This question can be answered based on what we know about zoology, the scientific study of the behavior, structure, physiology, classification, and distribution of animals and the animal life of a particular area or time. "Fossil evidence shows that such a creature did exist, 1 to 9 million years ago" (Harris 2021). Scientists called this animal Gigantopithecus, and it "was native to what is now central and southeast Asia" (Harris 2021). Not much is known about Gigantopithecus, "except that it was larger than a gorilla and had teeth similar to humans" (Harris 2021). Mark Strauss (2016) explains that "Gigantopithecus was pretty darn big" and that "fossils indicate it stood as high as 10 feet and weighed up to 1,100 pounds." When looking at evolution, "Gigantopithecus is most closely related to the orangutan, the only modern Asia ape" (Harris 2021). Considering this scientific information, "the most likely explanation" of this creature (if it does exist) would be that it "is a direct descendant of Gigantopithecus" (Harris 2021). Since we know now that Gigantopithecus did exist, and there is no evidence that primates evolved here, just how did a descendant of Gigantopithecus wind up in North America? Some primate fossils that have been discovered in America have turned out to be the oldest fossils ever unearthed in Europe and North America. These particular fossils indicate "that the creatures travelled from Asia to North America across the Bering land bridge between Siberia and Alaska, and then later journeyed on to Europe across another land bridge linking North America to Greenland and Scotland" (Marris 2008).

The orangutan, Gigantopithecus's closest relative and likely a close relative of Bigfoot, shares similar characteristics to those in many Bigfoot eyewitness encounters. Harris (2021) shares these orangutan characteristics that are in line with what Bigfoot eyewitnesses report, such as long, reddish-brown hair, highly intelligent, exhibits curiosity, occasional call to other orangutans, and being widely dispersed in their environment. Until we have tangible proof, the debate will continue.

CHAPTER 6
Goodway

REGARDLESS OF WHAT YOU THINK THIS CREATURE IS, THE SIGHTINGS down here continue to occur. On the south side of Monroe County is a little place called Goodway, another Bigfoot hotspot. Old Stage Road turns to dirt and is on one side of Goodway, not far from Range, and there are just country roads on the other side. It's pretty typical of this area. My brother Stacey also grew up reading Bigfoot books and watching Bigfoot shows because, as I mentioned before, our mom has always been a believer, and it fascinates her. Stacey just happens to live in a remote area of Goodway with his wife and several children. He has told me stories before of hearing screams and howls late at night. He feels he can tell if one is close by from the way his dogs act or by the coyotes howling. They all go nuts, and then they get really quiet and spooky acting.

One particular night, the dogs started acting strangely. He and his wife just happened to be outside by a fire, probably thirty to forty yards from the woods behind their house. The crickets stopped, and the woods got deathly quiet. Out of nowhere, a pine cone came hurdling out of the woods at them and landed near their feet! His wife had had enough at that point and decided it was time to go in.

Stacey went late one evening to fill his corn feeders up in the woods when, again, it got quiet and still. He started feeling spooked, so he tried to hurry his business. As he finished, a rock, or maybe a limb, was thrown at him. He wasted no time getting out of the woods. At 6'7", he said his legs were going! I have looked around out there and definitely found some wide trails.

Just a few months ago, I received another call about a giant man-like creature in the woods. This encounter took place just off of Old Stage Road on the back side of Goodway. A man was driving on the dirt road and said it was late in the evening because he remembered the sun being in his eyes. As he approached a bridge going over a small creek, he noticed something in the ditch off the side of the road. At first, he thought it was a bush. He noticed it was reddish brown and then thought it was a dog or deer. No, it wasn't either. He let off the accelerator. It was definitely too big to be a dog or deer. Maybe a bear? Then, as the car slowly approached, to his amazement, the creature stood straight up and leaped across the road in one step!

"What the hell did I just see?" he asked me. "Never would have thought something like that was real!" he exclaimed. I reassured him that he wasn't crazy and that I would look the area over the next day. I got off a little early and got to the spot about lunch. There is an expansive swamp on the side that the creature was crouched down on and another one on the other side. I did find what looked to be foot impressions. I also found some flat areas in the grass that looked like feet. He seemed relieved after I told him of my findings, if only to know that he was not losing his mind. He doesn't travel that road much anymore. He takes a different route. This swamp just so happens to come within about a mile behind my brother's house. Another coincidence!

A few years ago, a married couple reported a creature of some kind crossing the road in Goodway, on the main highway. It happened late one evening as the sun was going down. Off to the side of the road, the couple spotted another reddish-brown creature. It was very tall and was standing behind a tree. The headlights on the approaching vehicle automatically turned on in the fading daylight, and the creature turned from the headlights and walked back toward the woods. The husband said there was no doubt about what he saw. His wife said she had no clue what she saw, only that she got a very eerie, evil feeling looking at it. There are tons of reports that describe this very feeling when looking at a Bigfoot.

43

CHAPTER 7
Smokey Crabtree

I AM GOING TO DIGRESS A LITTLE BIT AND TELL YOU A STORY THAT I think you'll find interesting. It was spring break 2010, and to my children's disdain, we decided to take an Americana road trip instead of the usual beach trip. I tried to persuade them that the water was too cold to swim in anyway, but for some reason, that didn't seem to matter. We were headed up to an old Missouri farm place just to see different country, but I told my wife that we were going to have to make a small detour to Fouke, Arkansas. So, with my children whining, we hit Highway 84 through Louisiana, enjoying the sights and headed north to Fouke.

Anyone who knows anything about Bigfoot has seen the famous movie I mentioned earlier, *The Legend of Boggy Creek* (1972). This 1970s documentary claims to be a true story based on the accounts of encounters experienced by some Fouke residents. Several of these residents gave on-camera interviews and even reenacted their stories in the film. My mom made me watch this movie when I was young, and it terrified me! So, quickly, it became one of my favorite Bigfoot movies of all time and instantly added Fouke, Arkansas, to my bucket list of places to visit. My wife, Kristy, laughed about the detour I wanted to take but reluctantly agreed, and we were on our way. Fouke had one road in and one road out of town. I only remember one gas station, one post office, and an old country market. It was a friendly, quaint little town, very much like our communities here in Alabama. They had a wooden Bigfoot photo prop that you could take your picture with, so, of course, we did. Next, we went to the local market, which had wooden floors and an array of merchandise that included Bigfoot items and vintage antiques. The salespeople asked us where we were from, as it was obvious we were from out of town. We told them and explained that I was a major fan of the movie. It just so happened that the lady behind the counter was actually one of the daughters of a woman who was in the movie. And it was one of the most terrifying scenes! As she was retelling her mom's story, I brought up the name Smokey Crabtree, a main character in the movie and the person who got all of the residents involved. She smiled and told us that he lived about five miles down the road and that we really needed to go and visit. She said that he liked visitors and even had a museum out behind his house.

My eyes lit up, and I could see Kristy just shaking her head. She started mumbling, "I guess we are going down the road to see this Smokey Crabtree." I was already walking toward the van in the parking lot. With Tristan and Morgan thinking I had lost my mind, down the road we went. His place wasn't hard to find, and it was right on the edge of Boggy Creek. We pulled up to the house, but unfortunately, Smokey wasn't home. Kristy said that she remembers looking at my face, and it looked like I had just lost my best friend. I was getting back into the van to leave when a white Cadillac pulled up to the house. It was Smokey and his wife! My expression then transformed to that of a kid on Christmas morning. I introduced all of us, and we went into the museum. They were very happy to see us and treated us with the utmost hospitality. They said it had been a while since they had had any visitors.

After looking around the small museum, Smokey started talking about the movie and telling some of the stories. He showed me the three books he wrote after the film was produced. Until this visit, I thought that Smokey Crabtree and the film *The Legend of Boggy Creek* were one and the same. According to his first book, *Smokey and the Fouke Monster*, that is not the case. Crabtree states that his purpose for writing this book "is to keep the history of the Fouke Monster on a truthful basis" and to try to help his small town get compensated for the wrongs that he feels he bestowed upon them (Crabtree 1974). He goes on to explain in this book that although the film listed him in the credits as a special consultant and was marketed as a true story, it was "loaded with fiction ... a gross exaggeration of what really happened in Fouke and that 50 percent of the footage for the entire picture was shot after he was fired from the project" (Crabtree 1974). Crabtree's next two books, *Too Close to the Mirror: The Continuing Story of the Life of Smokey Crabtree* (2001) and *The Man Behind the Legend* (2004), are continuations of his first—more stories of his encounters, his family, and his upbringing, all told from his point of view.

It didn't take long for Smokey and me to start swapping stories and comparing my Alabama stories with some of the things that had happened in Arkansas. He was very interested in the stories from around here, and it was uncanny how similar they were to what had happened in Fouke. It seemed as if it was some of the same behavior, and it really piqued Smokey's interest. He told me that they still had incidents there and that there had been a roadside sighting not too long before we arrived. Then they would go months and months with nothing. I could tell by being around him that Smokey was the kind of man that, if he didn't like you, you would know it quickly. Fortunately for us, he and his wife seemed to like us. Suddenly, he got quiet, stared at me for a minute, and said, "I have something that I'm going to show you that I just don't show to anyone. It's in the back of my barn out behind the house, but you cannot bring your phones or take any kind of pictures."

I got really excited and said, "Let's go!" As we entered the barn, there was a special room in the back. In this room was a cadaver of some sort. It actually had a little stench with it. And being in the medical field, I can absolutely tell you that this was a body and definitely the weirdest thing I had ever seen. It looked to be six to seven feet long or tall. It was lying on its back, and the head was missing. The fingers had been chewed on, as had some of the toes, probably by rats or squirrels, since this cadaver had been found in the woods by some hunters. It was covered with hair, with some of its tendons exposed, and its arms, being longer than its legs, were stretched out by its sides.

At first glance, this cadaver appeared to be a massive cat, but certain things didn't make sense. First, how were the arms that much longer than the legs? How were the legs lying flat like a person's legs would, and how could you ever get a cat to lie flat on its back? He told us that some hunters had come across the body in the woods in Texas. They reached out to Smokey and agreed to give it to him. He had an autopsy done, but all it revealed was that it wasn't human and that it died of pneumonia. It was also female. He said the government had tried to confiscate it several times, but he wouldn't let it go. All of us were in awe, including my wife. We had an extra kid along with us on this trip, and I can remember distinctly him looking up at me and saying, "Gee, Mr. Ashley, I always thought that Bigfoot stuff was baloney. Not anymore! I don't know if I will ever hunt again. Thanks."

We left the Crabtrees with a real sense of accomplishment. We will never forget their hospitality or what we saw in that barn. Smokey and I remained friends on Facebook and talked occasionally until he passed away about two years later. He would never know how that visit made our whole trip. To this day, my kids still talk about our visit with Smokey and what they saw in his barn. They are actually glad that we skipped the beach that year. Unfortunately, that was our last trip we all took as a family.

A couple of months later, Kristy was diagnosed with a brain tumor called a glioblastoma. There is no cure, and therefore, it is ultimately a death sentence. It was the hardest thing I have ever had to handle or deal with, and it changed all of our lives forever. No combat zone in the world could have prepared me for what I was about to endure. I am so thankful today that we chose to take our little Americana road trip, take our picture with the wooden Boggy Creek Monster, meet Smokey Crabtree, and see that body, whatever it was, in his barn.

Here are the photos we took with the Boggy Creek Monster:

Kristy

Tristan

Morgan

Ashton

Ashley

Power Pig radio station in Evergreen, Alabama

Bigfoot statue in Evergreen, Alabama
Evergreen, the Bigfoot Capital of Alabama

CHAPTER 8
The Power Pig

A COUPLE OF YEARS LATER, AFTER KRISTY PASSED AWAY, GOD SENT ME a fantastic woman named Jessica. Although she is not a Bigfoot believer, I decided to marry her anyway. Shortly after marrying, we bought a little hardware store here in my hometown of Excel. Soon after that, we were blessed with a little bundle of joy named Leah, hopefully to be my caboose. Yes, I have a lot of children, and I will probably never be able to retire!

I wanted to add some hunting and fishing items to our new hardware store, which had previously been just that—a traditional hardware store carrying only household maintenance items, PVC pipe, fittings, nuts, bolts, screws, and paint. We were also adding miscellaneous home décor items, personalized items and gifts, candles, and of course, a Bigfoot section! Since we were introducing new items, we decided to change the name of the store to McPhaul's Mercantile. A general store label seemed more fitting for us. Since the store had been closed for about a year before we purchased it, and with the addition of so many new things, we needed to get some advertisements out there.

I hired a man named Ricky, who had tons of experience, to help us in the store. Ricky had a brother named Luther, who just so happened to be the local DJ at one of the radio stations in Evergreen, called the Power Pig. Luther has been on the radio for years, and everybody listened to *The Morning Show*, which was very colorful. Many local merchants called in to talk about their businesses. So, we started advertising with the Power Pig. Before long, I asked if I could call in one day a week and maybe give a hunting report, just to talk about what people were seeing and killing, different tactics, and so on. To my surprise, they let me start my Wednesday-morning hunting report, and I really enjoyed it!

I actually received a lot of good feedback from my hunting report. The other host of the show was a guy named Lee Peacock, who just so happened to be one of my neighbors. He also worked for the newspaper in Evergreen and added a ton of enjoyable content to the show. Lee would always do a "this day in history" on the show, where he traveled to different parts of the counties, exploring local history and folklore. He also wrote tidbits about what he saw or found in the local paper, and sometimes we would discuss it on the show. Lee is a hell of a writer and an all-around good guy. With never knowing what Luther was going to say (he is a crusty Vietnam marine vet), they made a good team, and it made for good entertainment.

One afternoon, Lee got a call from a lady who was traveling on Highway 84, east of Evergreen. She said she saw a big, hairy creature cross the road on the Sepulga River. This encounter was in the daytime. Lee wrote about it in his newspaper, and the radio station was soon buzzing about it. He asked me off the air, after my hunting show one week, what I thought about it. I told him I would talk to him later that day in private, just me and him. So, later that evening, Lee came by my house, and we sat down in my game room. I unloaded on him. After I told him some of the stories, Lee's mouth was wide open, and he didn't say a word. I looked at him and asked, "Well?"

He just swallowed and said, "Ashley, if you say this, then there has to be something to it!"

I told him at the time I wanted to keep it secret, but eventually, we started talking about it on *The Morning Show* on Wednesday mornings. Next thing you know, it blew up. It quickly went from the hunting report to the Bigfoot report! I had people stop me in town and say that they stopped work on Wednesday mornings just to listen to the report. Then people would call me or stop by my store to tell personal stories and report some of the things that happened to them.

Now, at that point, I was starting to believe that maybe I wasn't crazy. I was starting to see a pattern with some of the sightings. I could not believe it had gotten as big as it did. I mean, how many of these creatures were out there? Most everybody I met either had a story or knew somebody with a story.

All of this activity eventually led to Evergreen being named "The Bigfoot Capital of Alabama." There is now even a Bigfoot statue in downtown Evergreen. A lot of the stories I am about to write were told because of people tuning in.

Even now, when I'm at work, prepping or talking to somebody before surgery, people look up and say, "Hey, you're that guy on the Power Pig."

I laugh and say, "Yeah, that's me." And sometimes they have a story of their own.

The railroad tracks that cross Drewry Road—also
where the huge, glowing orb was seen

CHAPTER 9
The Railroad Tracks at Drewry Road

THE RAILROAD TRACKS ON DREWRY ROAD IN MONROE COUNTY ARE A unique place, full of Bigfoot lore. Leaving Monroeville, going east toward Evergreen, you will cross some railroad tracks on Drewry Road. This is how you go to Evergreen the back way. These tracks have been associated with a lot of folklore for years. I have no idea why. One guy, a well-respected businessman, swore he saw some strange lights on these tracks at this crossing. One night, Tristan and I were traveling home from Pine Orchard and saw a large, glowing orb on these tracks. At this particular place, it is probably less than a mile from the Old Federal Road. We both actually thought it was a train, but we had plenty of time, so we pulled across the tracks and stopped. Tristan got out to get a drink from the ice chest on the back, and I asked him, "Son, where is the train?"

He came back, bewildered, and said, "Dad, there is no train." Then it dawned on me that the light we saw was not shining as much as it was glowing. To this day, I have no idea what it was. As I said, for some reason, there is a ton of folklore around these tracks.

There have been several reported sightings of creatures walking down the railroad tracks as well. I heard a rumor that an old woman who lives near these tracks said she witnessed Bigfoot walking across the field from her house with a deer over its shoulders, like it was a sack of potatoes. It was said she talked about it like it was an ordinary experience. The person who told me would not or could not give me any more details, and I have yet to be able to get in front of this lady to ask her myself.

I also know of a man who lived near these tracks for years and would tell people that these creatures were there and that they traveled these tracks. He had no idea why they followed the tracks, and he didn't care who believed him or not. He has passed on now, but I know his son, who is also well respected in this area. He told me that he remembered a time when he had a lot of hog dogs. Now, these dogs were hundred-pound bulldogs that would go in and catch wild hogs out of the swamps. These dogs didn't play, and they weren't scared of a thing. But he said he remembers distinctly one evening when he and his dad were near the tracks and heard a holler off in the distance. The dogs started acting funny. His dad told him, "These dogs ain't stupid. They know that means danger. Let's go back the other way."

One evening, I got called into the hospital to do an epidural on a laboring patient. This young lady was in excruciating pain, contracting hard, and ready for her epidural yesterday! You know they're ready when they're wiggling on the bed like something out of the exorcist. As I was introducing myself, she looked up at me and said, "Hey, you're the guy on the Bigfoot show." I laughed as she gritted her teeth and said, "Well, I have personally seen one!"

Caught off guard, I said, "A Bigfoot?"

She came back with a big, resounding *"Yes!"*

After the epidural, when she was quite comfy, she told me her story. One evening, she was traveling east on Drewry Road toward Bermuda, only a couple of miles from Langham Road. She was just crossing the railroad tracks when a large, hairy creature on two legs ran across the road in front of her. She said there was a truck coming the other way, and it had to go into the ditch to keep from hitting it. She said she had no idea how tall it was; however, she had to look up about as far as she could in her windshield to see the top of its head. She said it towered over the car. In a panic, she mashed the accelerator and went down the road for about a mile. At that point, she started shaking so badly that she had to pull off to the side of the road and call her mom to come get her to drive her home. Her biggest regret, she said, was that she didn't stop to talk to the truck driver who went into the ditch, to verify what they had seen. I wish I knew who was in that truck. Maybe he will call me after reading this book.

This is one of my favorite stories, because no woman giving birth is going to lie! No man on earth is brave enough to call her a liar at this point, I promise! A few months later, I got another report that added even more validity to hers. I was talking to a logger friend of mine, and he told me a couple of stories that he had. The first incident took place on a tract of timber that they were cutting up in Pine Orchard. He said one night it rained, and when they went back the next morning, there were footprints all over their freshly cut road. The prints were much bigger than a human foot and were stretched out on the road for quite a distance. He said his workers were a little scared to go back in there and work that day. The next story he told was that his dad saw a giant creature in the 1970s cross a road. It was the middle of the day, and it did not run across the road; it walked! His dad told him he had to sit there in amazement and just watch it walk across the road like it didn't have a care in the world. It was reddish brown, huge, and on two legs. Guess where it was? The railroad tracks on Drewry Road!

These railroad tracks are not far from Bermuda and literally ran right behind my grandparents' farm. They run parallel with the Old Federal Road for a ways. These creatures definitely seem to be sticking to some of the same paths.

CHAPTER 10
The Alabama River

As time went on, my understanding of the patterns and habits of Bigfoot grew with every account of a sighting and from some amazing stories I heard from people who aren't known as tellers of tall tales. If you travel west on Highway 84 in Monroe County, you will cross the Alabama River at Claiborne. This community began in 1816 and, after the Creek Indian War, became one of the busiest communities in Alabama. At one time, it was rumored that it would become the capital of the state, but disease, such as yellow fever, darn near wiped it out. The town was then moved a little eastward to what is today Perdue Hill, and Claiborne quickly became a ghost town. There are several reports from people hunting and fishing along the Alabama River, and there are several actually close to old Claiborne and Perdue Hill. This place is a vast area of timber and swamps that goes on for miles.

One story is from J. Dunn, whom I have personally known for years. I have been good friends with his cousin since grade school. We grew up within a bicycle ride from each other. I wanted J. Dunn to put his dad's story in his own words. I can tell you that Mr. Dunn was a no-bull-crap kind of man, and if he told you something, you best believe it. Here is his story:

> My father, D. Dunn, was an avid fisherman, hunter, and trapper. He survived the polio that he contracted as a boy and wasn't supposed to ever walk, but he did. No doubt he was tough. He was also hardworking and

no-nonsense. He was respected and known by many. Being that he was an avid fisherman, people would say, "If Don ain't catching any fish, you might as well stay home." His ritual every Friday during the summer months was to leave straight from work to the Alabama River at Claiborne Landing and launch his flat-bottom johnboat. He would run trotlines and boxes all night. You see, Dad would fish for extra money and for freezer food. He would return home Saturday morning around noon so that we could clean the fish and pack it for sale or for the freezer.

I gave you a background on my dad so you might understand why one particular trip stands out in memory for me. This was the early eighties, maybe '83 or '84, springtime before school let out. Dad left work as normal and went to the river and went South to Marshall's Bluff, which is south of the grain elevator. The water is always deep there no matter how low the river gets. It takes a little time to get there with a sixteen-foot johnboat with a thirty-five horse Evinrude full of gear. As usual, we did not expect to see him till sometime Saturday morning. This particular trip, he was back Friday night between eleven and midnight. The boat ride back to Claiborne and the trip home would've taken about two hours, and still Dad was noticeably pale and wild-eyed. He told me and my brother to go to bed, but I stayed up, down the hall, to listen to what was wrong as he spoke with Mama.

He spoke about being anchored out just north of the Bluff. He was reel fishing as the trotlines and boxes were soaking. It was a well-lit night, with the moon shining bright. He told Mama that he started hearing rustling noises on the bluff, like something huge running through the woods. Cracking limbs, snapping trees, and the ground shaking. It was so loud he used the spotlight to shine the bluff but saw nothing. He dismissed it until it happened again. He stood up this time to shine a little better when something let out a horrible yell like he had never heard before. He said all the hairs on his arms and neck stood straight up! Said it was so loud he felt it in his chest! [Sound familiar?] He said at that point he was still shining the light when something either jumped from the bluff into the river or something very large was thrown into the river. It created a huge splash not far from his boat.

At this point, he didn't feel safe anymore. He had had enough, so he jumped to the front of his boat, pulled the anchor, and headed to the landing and to home. Sunday morning, he and I went back and pulled all the lines and boxes from the area. I tried to talk to him about it, but he would just say that he didn't know what the hell it was and didn't want to talk about it anymore. Over the years, I would try to bring it up a little bit, but he would just scowl and give me the same answer.

That was always his answer until he passed away. I am an avid hunter and fisherman myself. I get it from my dad. I have hunted and fished all around this river and surrounding areas and creeks. I myself have had strange occurrences and have never forgotten my dad's story. It always made me extra cautious when any of these occurrences would happen. I believe my dad did have an encounter with a Bigfoot that night and that maybe he did see it jump from the bluff. And I believe that maybe some of my occurrences could be exactly what scared my dad all those many years ago in South Alabama.

I find it interesting that during the same time frame, almost in the same spot, but on land, a witness saw a road crossing. This story was told to me many years ago, but I remember it pretty well. I have a friend whose dad was a very serious person who worked for the telephone company. I never knew this man to lie about anything, and even if you thought he was, you probably wouldn't tell him. He came home from work one evening, grabbed a cold beer, and told us boys the story.

It was a stormy evening, and the phone lines went out near Perdue Hill off of County Road 1. This road runs parallel with the Alabama River. When he got to the folks' house, they rushed outside and told him to hurry inside. Being that the weather was bad, he quickly obliged. As he came inside to service the phone, they were very scared and excitedly told him that there was something out there, hollering and screaming. He didn't think much of it and figured it was just a panther or something; he told them that, whatever it was, it would probably move on.

He fixed their phone, and they thanked him and worriedly escorted him to his truck. He laughed to himself as he pulled out of the driveway. He went just a short way up the road when he saw what he thought was a bear on all fours. It was off in the ditch and just kind of looked as if it was crouching down. Wondering if he was seeing things, he started slowing down. As it came up in view of his headlights, this bear suddenly stood up on two legs and ran across the road! The head was well over the roof of his work truck. As he sipped his old Milwaukee Light, he laughed and very seriously told us, "It was no bear. It was a Bigfoot. I'm telling you, it was. And y'all can believe it or not! I don't care either way, but I know what I saw." He said for a minute he thought he was going crazy. "Those things aren't supposed to exist!"

One of the most compelling stories I have been told involves a video in this very spot off the Alabama River in Perdue Hill. I received a call from a gentleman named Wayne. I have known him for a while, and he really just wanted some answers. He is very well respected, and I have never heard a bad word about him. He was also very much a nonbeliever until one fateful morning.

Wayne was asked to help work on a camp house on a very ritzy hunting club just off the river. As he pulled up to the property, he noticed a big, fully grown doe on the pond bank in front of the camp house. He watched the doe for a few minutes, and eventually she disappeared into the woods behind the pond. That's when all hell broke loose. He heard a tremendous racket, like a fight, followed by hollers and screams that would make your skin crawl! Phone in hand, he started walking toward the noise, videoing. You can clearly hear the racket as he is getting closer. He accidentally hit stop and then resumed as he walked up on the deer. Once he saw what was happening, he accidentally hit stop again as he ran off. What he saw shook him to the core.

Standing in the creek behind the pond was an approximately six-foot hairy creature with his hands around the throat of the doe, holding her head under the water as the deer was fighting for her life! Now let me make a point here. Nothing, and I mean nothing, can do such a thing down here to a grown deer. If you don't believe me, go and grab a young eighty-pound deer that's been shot but is still half-alive and see what happens. It can whip the strongest man!

Wayne was stunned for a second, then remembered that he didn't have a weapon and took off back toward the truck. When I talked to him, he was obviously shaken up about what he had seen and kept reiterating that it was no bear. He wanted some answers and verification that he wasn't crazy, so I shared some of the other stories from the same area. I think maybe it helped him some. He told me that he had even lost sleep over the encounter, wondering what the hell it was that he saw.

With his permission, I sent the video to M. K. Davis, a video guru who has been researching the Patterson Sasquatch film for the last twenty years and has compiled one of the largest collection of images from this film (Davis 2020). Davis's findings were pretty remarkable. You can see the deer thrashing in the water as something moves toward it, reaching for it, as the video turns off. Also, what we didn't know, that Davis was able to enhance, was that there was another creature on the bank watching the whole show. Good thing Wayne didn't stick around. When I showed him this, he said it gave him chills. The big creature on the bank looked like an eight-hundred-pound gorilla. What was it doing? Teaching a young one how to hunt or kill a deer? I don't know, but I do feel this could have turned into a very dangerous situation very quickly!

Wayne called a friend to go back over there with him, and when they got there, the deer had actually survived. He said that the deer, panting very heavily, was standing under a waterfall coming off the pond to cool off. It eventually hobbled back into the woods.

There were several encounters with Bigfoot that took place up along this river. Again, near Perdue Hill, I know a gentleman, whom I will call Ryan, who had a hunting camp here several years ago. This was very close to the time of the telephone repairman story. I had always heard rumors of this story but just recently ran into Ryan himself, and he was happy to tell me his tale. He had a small camper trailer nestled deep in the woods near a swamp just off the Alabama River. Ryan had been there for a few days, camping and eating gourmet foods, such as Vienna sausage, spam, and pork and beans. Friday night came, and a poker game had been planned on his remote spot in his camper, which had no running water and electricity that was supplied by a generator. For the poker game, Ryan and his friends decided to smoke a hog outside in a pit. They started it early, so by evening, the hog had been smoking most of the day. The drinking commenced, cards were falling, and the laughter and stories were abundant. In the middle of the poker game, Ryan said all the bad food and drinking from days prior caught up to him. His stomach rumbled and churned, sending him tons of cramps and telling him it was time to go. Because it was freezing that night, Ryan was wearing coveralls, which is a jumpsuit type of insulated, protective clothing some hunters wear when it is really cold. He tore out of the camper, unzipping his coveralls, as he ran toward the edge of the woods, where he crouched down, coveralls around his ankles. As the explosion was in process, a large hand from behind grabbed his shoulder. Ryan said he distinctly remembered looking down and seeing the arm covered in hair as thick as matchsticks. At this point, he took off running back to the camper, screaming as he was pulling at his coveralls once again. Covered in some of his business, he burst through the camper door, hollering that something was out there. The guys quickly noticed that Ryan was filthy, and it ended the card game for the evening.

Ryan said he has always stuck to his story and that the guys gave him a pretty hard time, especially since no evidence of the encounter was found anywhere outside—that is, until the next hunting season when one of the guys had an experience hunting over a food plot close to the camper. As dark approached, a towering, hairy beast lumbered across the back of the food plot. When the guy returned to the camp, he was stuttering to the others about what he had seen and that it had to be a bear even though it lumbered on two legs. The poking and making fun of Ryan stopped after that evening.

I heard another very similar story, but it happened on the other side of the river. A woman told me that her dad went hunting one day and had to take a nature call in the middle of the woods. All he had was a shotgun. I believe he was turkey hunting. As he was doing his business, one of these creatures came up behind him and started growling. Falling down in his own poop, the man crawled off quickly, snatching his pants as he was crawling. He ended up getting into a small branch and swimming down the creek. He got turned around and did not come back home until the next day, all shaken up and extremely dirty. He went back to the area a few days later with about ten friends to retrieve his gun, which was still there beside the tree. Funny story to me, but it wasn't to the gentleman. He honestly thought he was going to die that day. So, if you're out and about on these old riverbanks late in the evening, you better listen and be alert. You never know what might be near or what might be creeping up on you!

Still image from Wayne's video of the deer drowning.
In the top center, you can see the gorilla-type creature at the bank.

Still image from Wayne's video of the deer drowning.
The deer is on its side.

Still image from Wayne's video of the deer drowning.
Next frame in the video. You can see a smaller creature
with an arm stretched toward the deer.

CHAPTER 11
The Growl

AM I A SKEPTIC? AM I BELIEVER? ARE THESE CREATURES EVERYWHERE? These were some of the questions plaguing my mind when this next story took place. I am honestly not sure what category I was in up to this point, but I was definitely aware that something was out there. A few years back, I was hunting on a club between Bermuda and Pine Orchard. Now, this land is owned by the same man I lease from in Pine Orchard. I am not big on hunting clubs, but I wanted to try a new area. This place is roughly ten to twelve miles from my lease and has dense trees, swamps, and creeks and no nearby neighbors. I also thought it might be fun for the kids.

I always do a lot of scouting before the season comes in. I like to find the food sources and trails so that I can have some success when it's finally legal to hunt. This time, I found a nice deep hardwood bottom on a little stream that was surrounded by young, planted pines. I set out some cameras on the oaks, and sure enough, I spotted a nice ten-point coming in as relaxed as could be.

Once bow season came in, the hunt would be on! But, just my luck, every time I set up on him, he decided to eat under a different tree that was just out of range. He either liked variety or just liked making me look dumb. Maybe both! I had him patterned pretty well and pulled out about a week before gun season to let him get comfy again. Bocephus and I were going to set up on him opening morning of gun season. Bocephus is my .308-caliber rifle. It is a customized Mauser action with a Kimber barrel and is like an extension of my arm. Very few deer

70

that have seen him have lived to tell about it. As a matter of fact, I am a believer that a .308 is probably one of the deadliest rounds out there and, with the right shot, can bring down any large game. Any large game that's supposed to exist, that is!

The evening before opening morning came, I hung my climber up in the bottom. I had that buck pegged. Bocephus and I were going to close the deal at daybreak. I signed my spot out and headed up the tree just before daylight. I had chosen a tall white oak that towered over the bottom, overlooking a stream. This was a natural travel area and choke point. I quietly scooted up the climber, probably twenty-five to thirty feet, and was a good fifty to seventy-five feet above the stream and trail. I noticed it was very still and quiet as I was walking in, which put me on guard a little bit. I tried to be extra quiet climbing to avoid spooking my deer. When I got to a good stopping point, I eased myself around and sat down. Daylight was just starting to break, so except for a few spots, the shadows kept me from seeing the bottom floor.

As soon as I settled in position, a low growl erupted directly below me! It growled again, this time louder, and crescendoed up in tone. Words cannot adequately describe this growl. It was long and deep, and I have never heard anything so guttural in my life. My hair stood straight up, and I eased Bocephus up, shaking and stunned. I remember distinctly taking the safety off as I did. This thing sounded too big for Bocephus to handle, but I was willing to try.

I could scarcely breathe as the guttural growl echoed again through the bottom. I was praying for daylight. *Where is this thing? I can't see it! Do I even want to see it?* Mike Humphreys, of the Gulf Coast Bigfoot Research Organization (GCBRO), has heard one growl like this, and he nailed the sound pretty well. He said it was almost as if you have a two-hundred-pound Rottweiler with an air hose in his ass, and suddenly the air is expelled into a giant drum, resonating a deep, guttural sound. As I was searching with my scope and eyes, I heard another hunter clumsily walking to a stand on the other side of the bottom. Most of the time, this would make me fuming mad, being that this is what I hate most about clubs, but that morning, I was OK with it!

We had this thing pinned, and it got quiet. My mind was still trying to find a rational source for the growl. Was it an old, gnarly buck that was grunting? Maybe a huge old boar hog? Maybe, but where did it go? I knew it had to still be there, so I kept Bocephus at the ready. Nothing! A few minutes later, I got down and made sure the other hunter could hear me. I looked for tracks but didn't find any. It didn't come past me. It didn't go toward the other guy, so it had to have gone out in the opposite direction. I have heard hogs and deer run out, and if it was either one, it surely would have made a commotion getting out of there with another hunter approaching. Whatever this creature was, it snuck out of these woods without a sound! This was not typical animal behavior, especially for one rather surrounded. I asked the other hunter if he heard the growling as he was walking up, and he didn't. But I promise, it was loud enough that he could have.

Whatever it was, I felt that I must have surprised it that morning. It watched me climb that tree, and when I got still, he didn't like it one bit. All I could come up with is that it was another monster, just like the one I heard on my Pine Orchard lease. Damn! Seems as if these damn things follow me!

CHAPTER 12
Theresa's Story

THERESA, A DEAR LADY AND FRIEND, TOLD ME HER STORY ABOUT AN encounter with Bigfoot years ago, and I felt compelled to include it. This story came up around a campfire one night, so when I began to work on this book, I called her to verify what I remembered her telling me. Her story is still the same as I remember hearing it years ago. A little beyond the Alabama River lies Choctaw County. It is in this heavily wooded and farming county where Theresa's grandparents lived. Approximately fifty years ago, when she was a young girl, she and her six or seven cousins went to stay on their farm. They had been playing outside the whole day and had a little fort they had constructed on the edge of some big pines in the backyard. Her uncle, who helped on the farm, had just told her grandmother not to allow the children to go down and play near the pond because it was dangerous. He had seen some footprints over there that unnerved him but did not elaborate any further. As it was getting dark, one of Theresa's cousins just happened to turn around, facing the woods, and started stuttering in a panic, shouting, "Booger man!"

When Theresa turned around, she witnessed a sight she has never forgotten. Fifteen feet away was a tall, hairy creature. Its hair was brown and sloped off the arms and the sides as it was staring down at them. She said it had a very ugly face, but she only glanced at it because they all took off running and screaming toward the house. They were rushed inside as they tried to tell their grandparents what they saw. Her grandmother quickly sent the girls to one tub, which was on the front porch, to bathe, while her granddad did the same with the boys on the back porch, with a gun in hand. All the girls slept in the living room that night, while her granddad stayed up with a gun, guarding the house.

Theresa remembers that night being a long and frightful one. Hollers and screams echoed outside, and the horses in the pen were in a panic, running all over the place. They did not like what was out there and did plenty of hollering of their own. She swears that at one time, she remembers this creature trying to get into the house. Neither the kids nor her granddad got very much sleep that night. She remembers the story vividly, and to her, there is no doubt that these creatures are out there!

As I thought of Theresa's story, I had a few questions. Just some things to ponder. If this had happened to me, wouldn't I have gone out there and investigated? Her grandparents never questioned any of them; they just took the kids to safety. It honestly makes me wonder if they didn't have a lot more stories than what Theresa knew about. I have a feeling it probably wasn't her grandparents' first encounter.

The GCBRO at a parade in Louisiana.
Pictured are Brandi Hamilton, Don, Jim, Mike, myself,
Brenden Hamilton, Bobby.
Brandi and Brenden are children of Bobby.

CHAPTER 13
The GCBRO

As I talked about earlier, the Sepulga River sighting that Lee Peacock reported caused quite a stir and a lot of talk around town. It was from this report that I learned of the Gulf Coast Bigfoot Research Organization, or GCBRO for short. Don McDonald, a GCBRO member from Mississippi, caught wind of this story and tracked down Lee Peacock at his newspaper office. Don wanted to know more about the area and other sightings or reports from around here. Of course, Lee obliged with some of the reports and gave Don my number.

The only thing I knew about these guys was that they had a TV show on the Destination America channel that was called *Killing Bigfoot*. I actually remembered watching one of the episodes about a year earlier and really liked it. The group would go out and investigate reports from people who were having problems with these creatures. They would try to hunt the property and help the people in distress. This was right up my alley, but I had no idea if it was real or if it was all just for show. To be honest, I was a little leery of any Bigfoot groups.

Don called me after his conversation with Lee. I told him about the man scream that I heard around the same time as the Sepulga River sighting, as well as some of the other things that had been experienced in Pine Orchard. He decided to make the trip to Alabama along with another GCBRO member, Mike Humphreys. Several weeks later, Don and Mike arrived in Evergreen. Lee and I met them at a local restaurant for lunch to get acquainted. We discussed some of the reports about sightings and experiences that had been happening in the area. These included the Sepulga River sightings and stories of Pine Orchard and Langham Road. We compared them with stories from Mike and Don and their experiences with the GCBRO. Most of their accounts were very similar to ours here in Lower Alabama. They were definitely interested in seeing more. As soon as we finished our meal, Don and Mike wanted to go explore the Pine Orchard area, so off to Pine Orchard we went.

On the way, we drove through Bermuda, and I was able to show them areas in which sightings had taken place. Don was a likable person. He liked to joke around a lot and was easy to get to know. Mike was kind of quiet and mostly just looked and listened. I was impressed by them because they seemed normal. And, like me, not everything they heard or saw was a Bigfoot. Actually, they seemed very skeptical of any story or sighting. If it could be explained a different way, that's what they went with. I took them to a man's house in Pine Orchard where allegedly tons of activity had occurred. Don and Mike were very polite and respectful, even though some of what the man told was probably a far stretch from the truth.

The next day, Don spoke at the Evergreen Collard Green Festival. There was a room full of adults and children. I was amazed at how many people showed up to hear Don and how many people in the room had had some type of sighting or experience. Most of the folks in the room just wanted some answers and verification that these things are out there. Yes, the Collard Green Festival is real, and so is the Sausage Festival. They are both held annually in Evergreen and are a blast!

I probably spent two to three days with Mike and Don, and I can tell you that I learned tons. They answered several questions that I had about what kinds of evidence to look for and certain sounds to listen for, and they both seemed to really like the area. Before they left, they came up with two conclusions. First, there were definitely creatures in this area. And second, they wanted a GCBRO member in this area to help retrieve stories and be a part of their hunting team. After getting the greenlight from Bobby and Jim, I was in. But I still didn't have any clue about what I was in for.

The GCBRO hunt team consists of nine members: founder, Bobby Hamilton from Texas; cofounder, Jim Landsdale from Louisiana; Don

McDonald from Mississippi; Mike Humphreys from Oklahoma; Tug Humphreys from Oklahoma; Barry "Bear" Schockemoehl from Oklahoma; Rogan Bird from Louisiana; Mike "Little Mike" from Oklahoma; and myself.

All of the GCBRO men combined have probably more than thirty years of experience dealing with this creature. What I find really cool and helpful is that a lot of times, different stories from different parts of the country come together and fit like a puzzle. This helps to provide a clear picture of these creatures—as clear as it can be anyway. Our group talks almost daily, but not all of our conversations are about Bigfoot. They range in subject, to say the least. However, if Jim is in charge of the conversation, it's mostly about the weather.

Bobby Hamilton was introduced to Bigfoot at a pretty young age. As he got older, he became a professional wrestler out in Texas and wrestled some big names. You would recognize a lot of them in the WWE today. Bobby and his brother were almost abducted by some of these creatures that used to come outside their window at night. The stories he can tell give you chills. He agrees that these creatures are not friendly at all and can be very dangerous. Bobby has several children who are also on the *Killing Bigfoot* show, and every one of them has had their own experiences as well. One of his sons, Brady, reports having a four-wheeler he had been riding snatched back by one of these creatures, to the point of bogging it down as if in mud. When Brady was finally able to break free, the four-wheeler shot forward like a rocket. Bobby is a very genuine, nice human being. He's very polite and respectful to everyone, but you do not want to encounter his bad side.

Jim Landsdale is a Vietnam vet and another nice guy to meet and talk with. Several years back on his property, called Monster Central, he had several of these creatures create a lot of destruction. The stories are endless on this piece of ground. A lot of people consider Jim the stubborn one of the group, but I really like him. He doesn't mind telling you what he thinks. I actually respect that in any person, whether I agree with them or not.

Members Mike Humphreys and his brother Tug are some of my favorites. Their experiences with these monsters are unparalleled. They are just down-to-earth mountain men, rugged and quiet, but they will do anything for you if they can. Another Okie boy in the GCBRO is Barry "Bear" Schockemoehl, and he fits the same category as Mike and Tug. Usually, if one of them is around, the other two are close by. They all have their stories, and Mike and Tug have been dealing with these things for years. You can actually read about Mike and Tug's experience if you Google "The Siege at Honobia." Some of the stories that these guys have about these creatures, and how they act or hunt, will blow your mind. Again, no one completely understands them. There are no experts. But everybody in this group agrees the only way to understand one is to have one, whether alive or dead. And none of these guys pretend to be experts, which is what I really respect.

Mike ("Little Mike") and Rogan Bird are two GCBRO members I met only once, but I can already tell you that you won't find any nicer guys. I camped with all of them down here, and it was a blast. The last member besides myself is Don McDonald. Don lives the closest to me; therefore, I work with him the most.

Overall, I can tell you that the guys on this team are very serious about what they do. They honestly want to help people who have problems. They really want a better understanding of this creature. And just to note, they all really hated the name of the show, *Killing Bigfoot*. That is not what they are about. I have been on some hunts with these guys and can tell you firsthand, it's for real.

Most folks we have talked to or investigated, from Louisiana to Alabama, do not qualify for GCBRO to come in and hunt. The people who do are in a sheer panic because they are scared for their kids, their pets, or their livestock. They don't know where to turn. Seeing the relief on their faces when we tell them, "We believe you, and we're going to try to help you," is a great feeling. It's a hell of a relief for someone when somebody else tells them, "You're not crazy." The people seem very grateful when we arrive.

My first hunt with these guys took place in north Georgia, based on a report that Bobby received. It was a beautiful, small piece of property nestled in the hills, owned by a retired marine gunnery sergeant who was a former jungle warfare instructor. He had a young, beautiful wife and a good-looking family. I will never forget what this retired marine told us. He said, "In my opinion, these things have always been here with man. But as man went more toward civilization, these things went deeper into the woods. They have learned how to adapt and survive and are the ultimate survivalists. If I had a platoon full of these things, I could take over any nation I wanted to!" I believe the gunnery sergeant was right. We did not get to do as much hunting as we had planned to on this property because the weather got so bad. But you should have seen the massive trails that went toward his goat pen—so wide a four-wheeler could fit down them. I was able to get up in a tree for a couple of hours before the weather got too bad and did experience some activity. I distinctly heard footsteps behind me, walking back and forth on two legs, as if trying to get my attention. I just stayed still. Aggravated that I wasn't moving, I guess, something was thrown that buzzed by my head close enough I was able to feel the wind off it. Keep in mind that I was thirty feet up in a tree. At this point, I decided it was time to go, just as the bottom fell out with the rain.

When we left, this family was very thankful for our visit, even though there was not a lot that we were able to do. Months passed, and the wife told Bobby that the place had definitely gotten back to normal. Her husband, the retired gunnery sergeant, recently passed away. Our prayers go out to this family in hopes that they continue to experience only peace on their property.

Some of the reports I get can be disturbing and really make me want to pull out my hair. It can be very frustrating. I never know what I'm going to drive into. Although the people are usually extremely nice and sincere, everything they see and the slightest limb break is Bigfoot. It is almost as if they live in constant fear of these things. In our opinion, most of these people probably did have at least one experience, and because of that experience, everything they see is Bigfoot. I guess I really can't blame them. All we can do is try to reassure them that they're going to be OK and try to come up with some things they can do to help them feel safe.

My wife, Jessica, and Ashton, my son, have gone with me a few times on these investigations. I must say, even though Jessica isn't a believer, she usually hangs in there and supports me. Just one of the things I love about her. I could go on and on about GCBRO and what we do. The stories are endless. I'm glad to be a part of the group, and our story is not finished by a long shot.

Rogan, myself, and Don after a hunt.

The GCBRO at my camp.
Pictured from left to right: Bobby, myself, Ashton,
Brady, Bear, Don, Mike, Little Mike, and Tug.

Downtown Burnt Corn

CHAPTER 14
Burnt Corn

WITH ALL THE OTHER STORIES FROM BERMUDA TO PINE ORCHARD, IT IS no surprise that there have been many encounters here in Burnt Corn. One of my favorite towns out of anywhere I have been is Burnt Corn, Alabama. Again, this is right off of the Old Federal Road or County Road 5. It is in between Bermuda and Pine Orchard and, according to Wikipedia, was established before Alabama was even a state. There is a lot of history here, including being the starting place for the Creek Indian War. When I was traveling with the military and homesick, I would always see the beautiful town of Burnt Corn in my head. It is an old town with buildings and churches that haven't changed since the early 1900s. There are quite a few Bigfoot stories here as well. Being in the remote area of the Old Federal Road and having a tiny population, it's no wonder this mysterious creature enjoys the Burnt Corn area.

One of the most intriguing stories from this town comes from a gentleman who actually lives downtown. Mr. Norman, being very well respected in the county and maintaining a high-profile job, settled here recently with his lovely wife and small child. He told me that one night, before a storm moved through, he heard what he thought was a tornado siren sounding off close by.

Mr. Norman, being new to this area and concerned, called a neighbor to ask if Burnt Corn had such a siren. The neighbor laughed and said Burnt Corn had no such thing, and he had no idea what Mr. Norman was hearing. A few days went by, and his wife's younger brother came for a visit. He was probably around fourteen at the time and was staying all weekend. It was getting late one night when they heard a commotion underneath their house. This is an older house, probably built in the early 1900s. When they went outside to investigate, they realized that there was a cat underneath their house.

They found this very odd, considering they had a couple of dogs in the yard, but the dogs were paying no attention to them or the cat. They figured the dogs ran the cat underneath the house, even though the dogs were strangely quiet and shying away from the area. Eventually, with flashlights in hand, they ran the cat out from underneath the house. The dogs still ignored the cat. They didn't even attempt to chase it. Again, strange. They all went back inside, except for the brother-in-law, who lagged behind with a flashlight. As he was coming to the front of the house to go inside, his light beam shot across the road, and he saw a giant creature standing under an oak tree watching him. It had red eyes that glowed in the light beam and was probably not even fifty yards away across the street.

They locked eyes for a few seconds. Then the monster just snarled, turned, and walked away, as if in no hurry and as if he was never there. The boy said it didn't run but cleared the whole area in about four steps. Terrified, the boy damn near broke through the wooden screen door on the front of the house, hysterically yelling for his sister and brother-in-law to lock all the windows and doors. There was not much sleep to be had in the Norman house that night.

Morning came, and the Normans decided to explore the area across the road. First, they measured a limb on the oak tree where the creature was standing. The boy said his head was almost to the limb, which measured ten feet off the ground. On the backside of the property, they found a wide trail coming up to an old house that is part of a hunting club. It just so happens that they dump a lot of the deer carcasses and waste back behind the old house. Mr. Norman says that his brother-in-law has never lied and has always stuck to the same story. The boy also said he could not believe how easily something that big moved across the ground. Lastly, he said he knew that creature was in total control of the situation.

This was in the summertime, well past hunting season. Was this monster used to coming up here to feed on leftover deer carcasses? Was it hungry and chased the cat underneath the house? Is that why the dogs acted strangely? I believe this thing was probably looking for a meal. Good thing the boy ran!

Just three to four miles behind Mr. Norman's place, another encounter took place that was equally as intense. Lee Peacock received a call and contacted me about a gentleman in Burnt Corn named Marcus who videoed a Bigfoot while hunting. Of course, I went out to visit.

It was during deer season, and Marcus had decided to hunt for some fresh deer meat across the road from where he lived. He sat down, gun on ready, and waited. It wasn't long at all before he heard some noise. This was a strange noise that sounded like an animal that was walking on two feet, not four. He thought he saw something step behind a tree in the distance, so he pulled out his phone and started videoing. You can hear Marcus breathing heavily as the video shakes, and suddenly you can see something come out from behind the big tree.

A huge head and shoulders start to emerge as Marcus tears out of there on foot. From this point, it looks like something from that movie *The Blair Witch Project* as Marcus hauls butt out of the area, cursing the whole time. That part of the video was actually pretty humorous, but I don't blame him one bit. Marcus, who is a pretty good artist, drew exactly what he saw on a piece of paper, and I can tell you it was quite impressive.

I also talked to his relatives who live right there across the street, all of whom have some kind of story. Most said that they could hear it hollering and screaming and snapping trees at night. One lady told me that she would not even walk to the mailbox in front of her house by herself. If she was by herself, she got in her car and drove thirty yards up the driveway just to get the mail. It was heartbreaking to me that this lady lived in such fear that she wouldn't go outside her home alone. I was also told that one winter, after a sizeable snowfall, which is pretty rare around these parts, huge tracks and naked footprints were found in the backyard.

Lee also went out and talked to these people, and all of their stories were the same. These are very quiet people who probably wouldn't talk to anyone else. I tried to get in touch with Marcus before writing this book but lost his contact information. I would bet there are more stories to add by now.

Lee found out recently, from an elderly lady who grew up in Burnt Corn, that some of the area between Burnt Corn and Pine Orchard used to be called Booger Bottom. She didn't know the history behind the name but stated that, as a child, she would hear terrifying stories about how children would go missing when walking at night near the road close to Booger Bottom. No one, she said, would be on that road at night. Even as a teenager, she was terrified to go near that place after dark. Now, whether the booger was one of these creatures or a deranged human being, I guess we will never know. But we can sure speculate! I have pretty much been here my whole life and had never heard this story. But it sure makes sense, especially with everything that we know now. Booger Bottom is only a couple of miles from where I hunt in Pine Orchard.

There are tons of hunters around here in this area, and I have heard stories that go back years—tales of being followed while walking out late in the evening, shining flashlights or headlights and seeing something huge standing behind a tree, and tons of hollers and screams that people can't make sense of. One year, some hunters from Florida came up here on a paid hunt. They were hunting off the edge of Burnt Corn swamp, and they ran out early one evening, hysterical, saying that something was in that swamp, hollering and screaming, and it wasn't like anything they had ever heard. I thought this was worth mentioning because these guys had no idea of the folklore here, and they paid good money just to end up coming out of the swamp early.

I have a good friend named Hilton who lives near here and grew up on Burnt Corn swamp. Hilton is a great guy with a respectable job, pushing retirement age. He said he can remember as a young kid fishing and swimming in Burnt Corn Creek, on several occasions coming across massive footprints that would spook him and his friends out of the bottoms. He knows some farmers whose cows were mysteriously killed and whose calves went missing. He has heard this creature scream on occasion, off in the distance, and one night, traveling on the back road from Evergreen, he saw one standing beside the road. He said it was standing under a giant oak tree off to the side of the highway, and unless a moose had moved into Lower Alabama, there was no way anything else down here could be that big. When his headlights hit it, it just kind of stepped farther behind the tree. Hilton said that a lot of the elderly people who grew up here have several stories, but just as I have encountered numerous times, they won't talk about it.

Historic marker near Burnt Corn

Downtown Repton

CHAPTER 15
Repton

BY THIS TIME, I WAS BECOMING MORE OF A BELIEVER. BEING IN THE GCBRO and hearing all the tales and lore made me want to dig deeper. Since my Wednesday-morning call-ins on the Power Pig, reports were starting to bleed in to Lee and me. And this is one that stands out. East on Highway 84, just outside of Monroe County, you will drive through a little town called Repton. This is on the outskirts of Bermuda, and Burnt Corn Creek crosses the highway just outside the Repton town limits. Near here is a family I have gotten to know well over the last couple of years. They have also experienced their fair share of Bigfoot activity and encounters.

This family's history with this creature started in the early 2000s when a grandfather was driving his three granddaughters home from school. So, the time of day would've been around three thirty in the afternoon. As they were on the dirt road to the grandparents' house, a big, hairy creature had jumped the fence and was walking on two legs in the middle of a twenty-acre cow pasture. This pasture, owned by a man I'll call Farmer John, was very close to the grandparents' house. The three girls and the grandfather were in shock as they watched the beast lumber across the pasture. It was clearly unafraid and in no hurry whatsoever.

The grandfather stepped on the gas to make it to the house, where he hurried the girls inside. The girls said their grandfather rushed through the door, grabbed his gun, and quickly drove back to the area. The creature was gone without a trace, but it left an everlasting impression on the family that is remembered to this day. They still live in the same spot and therefore drive by the cow pasture often.

I found out about this encounter because of the Wednesday-morning Bigfoot Report. One of the family members, Miss Loretta, heard the Bigfoot report and came to my store to tell Jessica to call me because she had some great stories to tell me. I was very intrigued, to say the least, and have developed a great friendship with this whole family. Again, they live on a very sparsely populated dirt road about three miles from Burnt Corn Creek.

Miss Loretta told me that she heard the creature holler and yell several times from their backyard. I told her to go to Walmart, buy a cheap voice recorder, and hang it up outside in a tree. She was able to get several recordings of what sounded like pretty legitimate screams. Some were coyotes, probably a lot were coyotes, but there were some sounds on her recordings that definitely would make you scratch your head. They could have very well been from the creature.

Behind Miss Loretta's house is a murky, snaky swamp area, and in front are open pastures with a pretty set of hardwoods and a nice beaver pond. On the other side of the road is Farmer John's cow pasture, where the grandfather and granddaughters encountered this creature crossing, with more hardwoods and another large beaver pond.

I met up with Miss Loretta's brother Steven, who showed me around the property. I didn't find much at first, but I did come across some odd things. As we entered the swamp, we immediately found a couple of possible impressions. A few minutes later, not far from the impressions, we found a child's stuffed animal. It was perfectly intact and fairly clean, clean enough in fact that I would not have hesitated to hand it over to one of my children. What made it odd is the fact that there are no small children in this immediate area. There are also no dogs. It seems as if no one is able to keep a dog around. But if it were a child, why on earth would a child be out here in the middle of this snake-infested, swampy place? And if it had been a dog or an animal that placed the stuffed animal out here, how was it intact and clean enough that I wouldn't think twice about immediately giving it to my child? We also found an old portable telephone in the same area as the stuffed animal.

Miss Loretta and her family told me stories of how they would build fires in their backyard and would hear howls and other strange noises. One night, Steven and Miss Loretta were sitting outside by the fire, listening to the howls, when they heard a strange whistle. Then a rock was thrown. It crashed on the side of the shed, and they took no time getting back to the house. They were very shaken up. The wood line from the shed was at least seventy-five yards. Being that I was now part of the GCBRO team, I decided to reach out to Mike, Don, and Bobby. I wanted Miss Loretta and Steven to be able to tell the guys about what had been going on around their homestead. I also wanted some guidance as to what I needed to be looking for, as all of this Bigfoot research was new to me, and I certainly didn't want to miss a thing!

Mike, Don, and Bobby recommended that I talk with the neighbors. Across the woods from Miss Loretta's house was another old house a young couple was living in. I pulled in and explained who I was and what I wanted. The young lady said that I was welcome to look around, but her expression told me she thought I was crazy. Honestly, I did feel a little crazy. I noticed, though, that she had completely fenced in her back porch and was housing all of her chickens and ducks on it. When I asked her why, she said something was getting them and that the fence was the only way to keep them safe.

The young lady went on to explain that some of her chickens and ducks had just disappeared without a trace. She also said that any dog they tried to keep just wound up gone or dead. Now, this got my attention, but I didn't show my sense of alarm as I looked around. I came across an old shed in the backyard and snuck a peek inside. Eureka! There was a whole room full of children's toys and stuffed animals. No doubt this was where the stuffed animal that Steve and I found came from. But how did it get to the swamp? From where I was to where we found the toy was a good five hundred to a thousand yards. A coon maybe? I'm not sure, but again, if it had been a coon, then certainly the stuffed animal would have been tattered.

One particular evening, Miss Loretta and Steve decided to build a fire and called me to join them to listen for anything strange. I did not expect to hear anything, but I went anyway. They had built a fire on the back side of the property, near a small pond at the edge of the swamp. I parked my truck up near the house, close to the dirt road, and walked to the back of the property to join them. We were just sitting around the fire, chewing the cud, when I heard trees snap up close to my truck on the edge of the woods. This was the same place in which a rock had been thrown, crashing into the shed several weeks before.

I didn't think much of it at the time, and no one else seemed to hear it, till a few minutes later when more trees snapped up the line, closer to where we were sitting. Now everyone was paying attention! Then limbs snapped, and trees shook again, even closer. I told everyone to stay cool and act normal when suddenly all hell broke loose. Whatever was out there came right up the tree line and got within fifty yards of us, shaking trees, snapping limbs, and making a stomping noise. You could literally feel the ground shake around us. No more staying cool! Everyone got real serious, real fast, and a couple of people cut and ran. The rest of us quietly and cautiously made our way back to the house. He won that night. One of Miss Loretta's cousins who was at the fire and ran when the ground began to shake was a nonbeliever. Now he's not so sure. He was pretty wide-eyed! After the fire incident, Miss Loretta was terrified to go out in her yard, especially with some of her small nieces and nephews who came over to visit. She was not sure it was safe and was a little worried. The creature definitely sounded aggressive that night.

One weekend, Don came over from Mississippi to camp out and look around. With perfect timing, Miss Loretta called me, saying she had found some tracks beside the dirt road on the edge of the cow pasture. When Don and I got there, sure enough, there was a footprint on the side of the road, along with some smaller footprints. You could literally see the toes. It was definitely a young one and a big one. Eventually, the GCBRO team came to look around and hunt Miss Loretta's property. The team that visited consisted of Bobby, along with his son Brady, Mike and his brother Tug, Don, Little Mike, and Bear. Unfortunately, we did not have any exciting encounters on this trip, but we did hear a really good bionic bird and found some great signs, such as a wood-knocking tree. A bionic bird is a whistle sound that a Bigfoot makes, similar to a screech owl but much louder.

The wood-knocking tree we found was off on the edge of the cow pasture. I saw that there were some scratch marks about four to five feet up a small oak tree. Another oak next to it had the same markings. Then I knew they weren't scratches; they were indentations. When I showed Mike, he knew right away and said, "Ashley, that's a wood-knocking tree!" He picked up a stick, hit a nearby tree, and sure enough, the mark it left was the same. It echoed through the timber. I remembered seeing some of these same indentations on trees in Pine Orchard and wondering at the time what had made them. Now I know. Even though we did not experience any live activity, we saw enough to know that these creatures were there. And it was probably for the best because, as much as I hate to admit it, Miss Loretta and her family fed us all with a lot of great southern cooking, and we were all too stuffed and therefore too sorry to hunt much anyway.

I remain friends with Miss Loretta and her family and continue to visit on occasion. She still has activity here and there, as do the others in the area. Farmer John, who owns the cow pasture nearby, had a cow locked up in a catch pen that somehow had its udders ripped off. He said he had never seen anything like it in his life and actually wound up having to put the cow down. Something had to have reached inside the catch pen and grabbed it. This is a hardworking farmer in his seventies, and in talking with him further, he admitted that his mother saw such a creature more than eighty years ago.

Farmer John lives on Burnt Corn Creek, which is where his mother had the sighting, not far at all from Miss Loretta's home. He said that late one evening, his mother was walking the dirt road near the creek when a large, brown, hairy creature stepped out in front of her in the middle of the road. It looked at her, turned around, and walked right back into the woods. His mother called it the wild man and always told that story as to why she would not let the children stay out late in the evening or go near that area at dark.

Farmer John claims to have never seen a Bigfoot personally, but he did tell a story to me, Bobby, and Brady about some young bears he had seen while on his tractor. He went on to explain that they were picking up freshly cut hay with their hands and smelling it. He said that eventually he heard the mother bear holler from the woods, and the young bears ran to catch up with her. Now this was on the edge of Burnt Corn Creek, and I will just let you think about that story for a moment ...

Tiny footprint inside a handprint or bigger footprint at Miss Loretta's

Another small footprint at Miss Loretta's

The knocking tree

Old dirt road on Burnt Corn Creek, where several sightings have occurred

Burnt Corn Creek/Swamp

Burnt Corn Creek crossing Highway 84

The old Masonic Lodge in Perdue Hill

CHAPTER 16
Frisco City / Perdue Hill

As it seems, most towns in Lower Alabama had stories to tell of encounters. The Power Pigg was starting to embolden people to talk. Frisco City is another small town in Monroe County. It is not very far from the river, and there have been several reports in this area through the years. I will tell you about just a few. I remember years ago, I heard from an old friend of mine who is a part-time taxidermist as well as a cop. He often hunted Bear Creek, a beautiful creek just outside of Frisco City, going toward Perdue Hill, that eventually dumps into the Alabama River. He clearly remembered seeing huge, naked footprints in the mud just outside the creek. That ended his days of hunting there pretty quickly.

Lovett Creek is another creek outside of Frisco City, off of County Road 10, that also dumps into the Alabama River. The creek is shallow but wide and beautiful. I heard the story of a man who put his son on a deer stand on this creek, and the boy claimed someone shot in the distance as he was sitting on his stand. Shortly after the shot, he heard limbs and branches snapping behind him to his left, which was downstream. As he turned toward the noise, a giant, hairy creature stepped out of the woods and walked into the middle of the creek, looking in the direction of the gunshot. Then it turned and walked back into the woods. The young boy was terrified and did not want to get down out of his stand. When his dad came to get him, he had to coax him down. He finally got him into the truck with the doors locked, and the boy was hysterical all the way home.

One of the best reports I received from this area was from a guy named Keith, who lives really close to Lovett's Creek. He was an army ranger and really didn't want to talk about his experience. I saw him at a local Christmas parade, and he asked me if I was still doing the Bigfoot report on the radio. When I said I was, I could tell something was on his mind. So I asked, "What you got going on?"

He smiled and then reluctantly said, "I think I have plenty."

Having grown up here, Keith knows the area better than anyone. His family settled in the Frisco City area many generations ago. He remembers, as a kid, finding a moonshiner deep in the woods near Lovett Creek. The moonshiner knew who Keith belonged to, so he gave him a bottle of fresh brew, telling him to give it to his dad. With two bottles left, the moonshiner went on to say that he was keeping one for himself and leaving the third for "Him." He told Keith not to tell a soul and that "He" would get his bottle out of the woods later. Keith took the bottle to his dad but always wondered who "Him" was.

Keith said there were many nights when he would be sitting out on the porch, and suddenly everything would just get unearthly quiet. Locust and crickets would stop chirping. He said the hairs on his head would stand up on end. He never understood the reason why until one day he and his wife were outside in the middle of the day and heard a loud scream across the road. The sound was so deep and loud that even the neighbors came out to see what was going on! It came from across the road, where Keith owns some private property with an old homeplace full of fruit trees and a pine plantation. This area backs up to a large parcel of timber belonging to a paper company. There are many game trails all around, with tons of hog signs.

Keith invited me out to his place to look around. As I followed him around the property, he started telling me of other stories that had happened fairly recently. He said he had trees pushed over for no reason, and a neighbor farmer had several calves go missing without a trace. I noticed a horse pen that looked fairly new. Some of the barbed wire had been pressed down, as if someone or something had fallen on it, but the fence line was clean. There were no limbs or brush that might indicate what happened. He then told me that they could not keep the horses in the pen. No matter the wire type, they would go nuts and break out. One day, a young horse went missing, so they just gave up and abandoned the idea of keeping the horses there. They had to find them another home.

Keith is a pretty quiet guy and was reluctant to talk about all this. He definitely has some kind of activity going on. And if I was a betting man, I bet it occurs mostly in springtime, because of the many fruit trees on his property. I believe the story has just begun on this property.

Another report came recently during a phone call to the Power Pig radio station. Luther took this call, which came from an elderly lady who lived in Chicago. She grew up on the road between Frisco City and Purdue Hill. As a nine-year-old child, after church one Sunday, she went across the road to a pasture to pick some plums. As she was bending to the ground picking up plums, she heard something walk up behind her. She looked and saw two huge legs but figured it was the bull that was in the pasture. She just kept on picking, and it got closer. She said it was making a strange noise, and then, finally, she looked up ... and up ... and immediately realized that it was not a bull!

She said it had wide teeth and snarled at her and smelled like several wet dogs and urine. She took off in a panic, screaming as this creature ran after her and actually pushed her through a fence. As it did, it tore a long gash down her back. She turned and took one last look as it yelled at her, but it stopped at the fence. She ran toward her house screaming. Her parents were out in the yard; they heard her and came running to help.

When she looked back, the monster had turned and walked away. Her parents met her in the pasture and brought her home to safety. She then felt the blood gushing out. Frightened, her parents called the small-town doctor who lived in the area. The doctor made a house call, gave the girl a shot of penicillin, and told her parents to follow up with him in a week.

The young girl was in shock and wasn't saying a word. The doctor told the parents not to worry, that she would come out of it, and that it was probably just a rogue bear. A couple of days later, the girl felt better, her wound started healing, and she started coming around and talking again. She said her parents questioned her on what happened and told her that it was probably a bear, but the girl insisted that it was not a bear.

She said it had two legs, two feet, and shoulders, and she will never forget the snarl and its teeth. Even as the lady was telling the story, she said throughout all these years, her story had never changed, and we could still hear her voice shaking as she recalled the events of that day. She said that she was glad that people in this area were finally talking about the creatures that live around here. She was glad to get her story out so that people would know that these things do exist and that they can be dangerous. She even has the scars to prove it! To this day, she states that she is still terrified and will not travel down a dirt road. Convince her these monsters aren't real!

The old Brushy Creek Methodist Church near Burnt Corn Creek
and Brushy Creek, not far from where the boy was ambushed

CHAPTER 17
Range / Lenox

ARE THERE ANY OTHER LOGICAL EXPLANATIONS FOR WHAT'S BEEN GOING on? I asked myself this question many times. I believe a bear is ruled out. It can't run across the road on two legs. It doesn't have shoulders, and it can't leap. However, standing up and being still, it could be mistaken for a bigfoot. Is a wild man or someone in a costume? Unlikely due to the randomness of the sightings and the size. Nestled close to Repton in Conecuh County are a couple of small communities. Range is the first and home to my camp, and then three miles up from there is Lenox. Burnt Corn Creek and Brushy Creek run right through the middle of these areas. Both creeks eventually flow into Brewton, Alabama, and then on to Pensacola, Florida. The hunting and fishing in these areas have been great for many years. And the Bigfoot stories from these areas go back generations as well. There was actually a *Mysterious Encounters* episode very near here that found hair that was later determined to have come from an unknown primate.

In the last couple of years, I have become friends with a guy named Rocky, who grew up in this area. Being a logger and in the woods every day, Rocky believes there's something to all of these stories as well and told me one of the funniest Bigfoot stories I believe I have ever heard. Rocky had two brothers working for him, and they were cutting timber on the Sepulga River just outside of Evergreen. They had cut a small wood landing, more like a small beach area, near the river and decided to bring a couple ladies with them one evening to party and, well, whatever. With a truck full of booze and two willing ladies, the brothers parked on the trail, and they all headed down through the woods to the private beach area they had cut out. The beautiful night was going great, with the mood just starting to get right, when one of the brothers decided it was time to replenish the booze. After retrieving some bottles from the truck, one brother turned on his flashlight to head back to the landing through the woods, and his light hit a creature in the middle of the trail that had red eyes and was tall and hairy.

Scared for his life, he ran past his brother and the two ladies and jumped in the river. Now he said he couldn't swim a lick but somehow made it to the other side, yelling, "Monster!" the whole time. He said it was an absolute miracle. The other brother, remembering there was a gun in the truck, ran back to grab it and wound up running right into the creature! It hollered, and he hauled ass, locking himself in the truck, leaving the two ladies huddled together on the riverbank screaming.

The brother across the river, still panicking, dog-paddled his way back to the other side, too scared to be by himself across the river. With the two ladies in tow, he started running toward the truck. The brother in the truck, who, by this time, was in a complete panic, started shooting out the window at their shadows. Luckily, he was a horrible shot and no one was injured, but he did manage to run the creature off, as there was no longer any indication that it was still there. The one brother said to this day that's the last time he was ever able to swim and, unfortunately, it was the last time they ever saw the two ladies!

More recently, Rocky told me of another logger's story. Log truck drivers get paid by their productivity, which is based on how many loads they haul in a day. It takes a coordinated effort between the drivers, loaders, and cutters. Some drivers who have been doing it for years have the skills to work on the loader and are able to load their own truck with the logs, which was the case in the following story. This motivated driver hit the woods early, way before daylight so he could load his truck and get an early start on his haul to the lumber mill. Between three and four in the morning, he hit the old logging road, again near the Sepulga River, going into the tall timber to load his truck. The moon was shining brightly as he approached. Logging roads vary in width, but he estimated that this particular road was ten to fifteen feet wide. As his headlights hit the mouth of the timber, a hulking, hairy creature emerged on the side of the road. With the truck's headlights getting closer to this creature, the beast came out in view and leaped across the road in one leap. This driver was so shaken that he did not load his truck up early that morning. Instead, he turned around and waited on daylight and for the rest of the crew to get there. To this day, he doesn't ever load his truck before daylight.

I ended up buying my own place out in Range from Rocky's family, a beautiful little fifty-acre paradise for hunting and fishing. I never expected to have or see any activity on it. One late night, my wife, Jessica, and I were sitting on the back porch of the old camp house when suddenly the crickets stopped. Deep in the yard, on the edge of the porch light, a huge, head-like object glided across the backyard. It stayed just on the edge of the light.

I stopped rocking in the porch swing, looked at Jess, and said, "Did you just see that?"

She said, "That weird glowing ball that just went across the yard? Yeah!" So, we both had seen it, but we had different interpretations of it. This is not uncommon with eyewitness reports. It is also something interesting to ponder. No doubt the object was round, no doubt it was large, and no doubt it was at least eight or nine feet off the ground and gliding across the backyard. I dismissed it as some sort of swamp gas, being as we are on the edge of a swamp, so I didn't think much of it after that.

Early one morning toward the end of deer season, I was sitting on a large pasture on the forty acres I lease right next to my property. The other side of the field is approximately 250 yards away. I got up before daylight, snuck into the shooting house, and patiently waited for the sun to come up. As the sun started to rise, the field began to become visible. However, the woods surrounding the field on the back side were still dark.

I was looking for deer on the edge of the light when something caught my attention out of the corner of my eye. As I started to focus on the object, it moved across the back corner of the field. It stepped out enough onto the field that I literally saw daylight shoot between its legs as it walked. It was on two legs and made three giant strides, then disappeared quickly into the dark woods. I saw the shadowy outline of the figure as it moved across the field, but it happened so fast it was very hard to focus on it completely. All I can tell you is that it was huge! It was very, very barrel-chested. It looked as if a Volkswagen was standing on its nose and you put two legs on the bottom of it! No damn wonder people think their gun isn't big enough. It's not! This monster, it's broad and thick.

But once again, I dismissed it and wondered, *Did I really just see that?* I continued to hunt, and when I got down off the shooting house, I walked to the other side, looked around, and found absolutely no sign of anything. Maybe the shadows were playing tricks on me. I don't know, but how do you explain the break in the daylight I saw? I was wondering if I was going crazy till a week later. I had a corn feeder in the backyard with a game camera attached to it. I went to check the camera one afternoon, and, strangely, no pictures.

Being a new camera with new batteries and a new sim card, this made no sense. I knew there had been a lot of deer feeding because there were tons of tracks under the feeder; there should have been hundreds of pics on my camera. Come to find out, even though it contained new batteries, the camera was dead. The batteries were dead. To this day, this makes no sense to me. As I was checking the camera, I heard a commotion behind the feeder on the edge of the woods. I walked toward the noise and found buzzards feeding on a young spike that had been coming to my feeder every evening.

I figured one of the neighboring hunters may have shot the poor thing, and it ran off down here and died. But something about this kill seemed strange to me. The hide was completely pulled off the ribs, and the deer's body cavity was completely cleaned out, and I do mean cleaned out. There were no organs or guts left, and there was not a drop of blood on the ground anywhere. The kill was fresh because the eyes were still intact inside the spike's head, and they still had some color to them. Whatever had gotten this deer left no clues. This deer was hollowed out like a canoe!

Later that night, I was asleep in the camp house when suddenly I sat straight up out of a dead sleep, thinking, *Oh my gosh, what if I did see what I thought I saw on that field, and it was hunting my feeder? What if that creature killed my deer? How would I know?* So, I decided to call Mike the next day and ask him.

Mike has personally witnessed these things kill deer and told me, "Ashley, usually the first thing that they will do is snap a leg."

I told him that I didn't remember a leg being snapped but that I would go back and check. So, I went back to check the deer and couldn't believe what I saw. The front right leg was completely snapped and twisted. Coincidence? I don't know, but this leg was perfectly snapped in two. *Damn!* I thought. The next day, I went to look at it again, and the carcass was completely gone. Not a trace. No drag marks either. So, figure that one out.

A year later, my son Ashton and I were hunting the property. I was in a climber in the swamp, and Ashton was at the camp house hunting off the top deck. He texted me and said he saw a ton of buzzards in the same area behind the shed where the deer was killed last year. Cursing, I told him to go check it out because I wanted to know if it was another deer. He did, but he didn't find anything, so he went back to his spot on the deck.

He saw a large buck walking across the other side of the field, so I eased down to see if I could find it since I was close. It was starting to get dark, but I had my good scope on Johnny Cash, my 45/70 Henry rifle. I also shoot heavy grain ammo, which will easily stop a deer, but just in case something else wants to come out, it would put a hurting on him as well. This gun, with that 400-grain ammo, would be an equalizer.

I did not see the buck, so I decided to head back to the camp. As I came across the pond dam, I scanned my thermal sensor in the backyard where Ashton said he had seen the buzzards near my shed. Looking for deer, I saw nothing, but as I moved my thermal to the front of the shed, I got a massive hit. I had the thermal on white-hot, and this literally looked like a full moon beaming through the trees just inside the woods. What was I looking at? I looked with my naked eye and saw nothing, but every time I looked through the scope, there it was! It was taller than the lean-to on my shed, which is about seven feet. This was nine to ten feet tall and huge!

I had the crosshairs on it and was easing my way toward it to see if I could get a better look. I had my finger on the trigger, but I could not positively identify what I was looking at. Growing up hunting, especially in the South, you never shoot something if you aren't 100 percent sure of what it is. I looked one more time with my naked eye, and when I pulled the scope back up, I literally watched this thing turn and walk away! My son Ashton had been ten minutes from walking within thirty feet of this thing. That put chills on me. The GCBRO hunt team, minus Rogan, came down and stayed at the camp. They found some huge trails and some impressions, and we heard a few knocks and whistles, but it stayed out of sight.

Behind my swamp, approximately a mile or two through the woods, of course, is Burnt Corn Creek. This place is fairly isolated, with only a few houses close by. There is one particular family that lives here that I've known for a while and pretty well. They are tougher than barbed wire and as honest as they come. As I mentioned before, Lee's article in the newspaper coupled with the new Bigfoot show on the Power Pig radio station had new stories coming in from all over this area. Turns out this family experienced several incidents and had quite a few stories to tell me spanning the last few years.

Just recently, a fourteen-year-old boy from the family was hunting very near the creek. He was walking out at dark with his flashlight when his light hit some huge red eyes standing behind a tree. When the light hit the creature, it quickly squatted down. Scared, the boy sat down with his rifle and his light. He said the monster started making weird sounds and started grunting and growling. It then started walking and running circles around the boy, popping limbs and trees! Terrified to move and with his dad away at work, the boy called his mom. She drove down the path and into the woods to get him.

To this day, he's very hesitant to go back to this area and will not go near it after dark. This would scare most grown men! This incident makes me wonder, What was this creature doing? What was it thinking? Was it trying to scare the boy off? Was it frustrated because he was sitting down, or was it contemplating an attack? I'm not sure, but I'm glad that his mom came and got him, and I'm sure he is too. He told the same story to Mike. The hunt team, along with myself, hunted this area, and while we did not hear or see anything, we did find a wide trail with some snapped tree limbs eight to nine feet off the ground, very close to where the boy was sitting. There was no doubt the boy was telling the truth. You could tell he was very frightened. His dad finally admitted that even he had been run out of the same stretch of woods a year prior. I'm pretty sure if I pried a little more, I could probably uncover many more stories from this family.

A few months ago, we had a fifty-year anniversary for my parents in Range. We probably had thirty to forty people at our little camp house, with some loud speakers and a sound system set up on the back porch. I remember making a joke that this was going to get the monsters stirred up! After most folks had gone home, and a bit after our preacher left, we started popping a few beers under the tent. It was just my two brothers, Jared and Stacey, Wes, my son Ashton, my stepson Eason, my nephew Trevor, and my dad. Old stories started to come to life as the beer flowed, and then a horrible stench filled the tent. It did not smell like wet dogs, as some have described from Bigfoot encounters, but it reeked of rotten eggs and sulfur, with some kind of a sewage aroma mixed in as well. Eason and Jared were outside the tent playing cornhole and also smelled this horrible stench.

Now, my dad is notorious for his gas. If he had a superpower, farting would be it! We all started moving away from him, asking what was wrong with him. Normally, he would brag if he managed to create a smell like this, but he was claiming his innocence. That convinced us it wasn't him. We started pointing fingers at one another, but each one of us claimed our innocence as well. We stayed outside talking and were hit by the foul odor two to three more times. I was starting to worry about a septic leak as the smell continued to come and go.

Finally, it was just Eason, Ashton, Wes, and me left at the house. I was sitting on the back porch when the smell hit me again, coming from the woods close by. Ashton and Eason walked out of the camp house and swore it had to be me. I promised it was not. The smell was strong and almost bad enough to make me gag. I came back the next day to clean and check my septic tank. No smell. No leak. I have not smelled it since, and I'm out here a lot! I did some research, and guess what skunk apes in the South are rumored to smell like? You guessed it, sulfur and rotten eggs! I guess our noise stirred one up, and he let us know how these creatures earned that name. Other animals can smell this bad, including hogs, but it certainly makes you wonder.

After a hunt, from left to right: me, Bobby, Brady, and Bear

Tree snapped near where the boy was ambushed in Range

Possible foot impressions in Range.

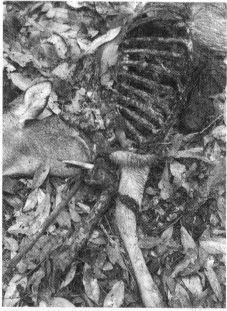

The deer killed behind my camp. Notice the snapped front
leg. The next day, the carcass was completely gone.

Foot impressions with toes in Range.

Wide trail with a structure behind my camp. Tug is in the background.

CHAPTER 18
Final Evidence

I HAVE MANY MORE STORIES THAT COME FROM PEOPLE IN ALL WALKS OF life. These creatures are part of our landscape here, just like the coyotes and cicadas. They have become part of our shared history. Just in case you are still not convinced, I will end this by offering a few more compelling stories. These tales are my final evidence that Bigfoot is real and that he is in Alabama.

Just south of my camp, going toward Brewton, there are many large creek systems, including Burnt Corn and Brushy Creek. Little Escambia is close by and almost follows the same path as those two. A local fisherman heard the Bigfoot report on the radio and got in touch with me about a startling discovery he happened upon while fishing Little Escambia. It was just after deer season a couple of years ago. He had loaded up his johnboat with gear and set out to put some fish in the freezer. There had been a lot of rain that winter, and the creeks were up a good bit. He rounded a bend and noticed there was a tall debridement pile of limbs stacked together. He thought it may have been caused by the flooding, but what he saw on top of the heap left him in shock. There were three deer stacked on top of one another in a nice, neat pile! How did this happen? Flood? Couldn't be. Bear? No, they usually bury their prey and come back for it later. A big cat? Maybe, but three deer? And all neatly stacked up? He couldn't make sense of it and decided to keep going. He said he did not feel safe in the area any longer.

I recently got another report, this time from a farmer in Bermuda, of five deer stacked on top of one another. This apparently is not too uncommon for these monsters. When the farmer went back the next day to investigate, they were all gone, except for one that was eaten clean! Mike Humphreys, from the GCBRO, said he has found dead coyotes stacked up neatly on top of one another as well. Guess they got too close. One can only speculate …

As I said previously, there were other sightings close by where I hunt. There are some brothers who live right down the road from where I hunt, and they have tons of stories. It's actually one and a half miles away, and a lot of our stories coincide. They have seen the creature and heard it on several occasions. They did not know what happened at my place, nor did I know what they had experienced until later. This adds some validity.

I killed a small buck one day and took him to the nearby processor in Pine Orchard. A young man grabbed the deer off the back of the truck, and we were making small talk. I didn't know him, and, to my knowledge, he didn't know me. He started telling me about a weird bear sighting he had had just a few days before.

It was late in the evening as he was traveling one of the lonely Pine Orchard roads near our hunting club. As he approached the bear, right before he got up to it, it actually stood up and ran across the road! I looked at him and said, "Ran?"

He looked sheepish and said, "Yeah, on two legs. It was crazy!"

I just laughed and said, "Friend, that was no bear!" He looked at me strangely and went back to work. Guess where it was? A mile behind where the brothers were living and just a mile and a half from where I was hunting.

Not long ago, I heard a story from a lady about my age who used to swim in a gravel pit near Lenox as a child. Her parents would take the kids for a dip in a gravel pit on weekends. There was one particular Saturday morning she says she will never forget. As they approached the swimming hole, her dad started acting concerned and worried. All around the hole, there were wide footprints, bigger than any man's! Hurriedly and to her dismay, he loaded the kids back up and went home. She said she has never forgotten that and wonders about those footprints to this day.

Jimmy is another person I have known for a long time who also grew up in Pine Orchard. I have actually known him since we were teenagers. I can't say I knew him very well, but he was always a nice guy and a fairly quiet person. Last year, Jimmy was traveling in his vehicle from his mother's house in Pine Orchard during the day at about 35 mph. These aren't great roads down here, and you certainly cannot speed in this area. As he was traveling, he watched a brownish, hairy creature walk across the road fifty yards in front of him. It ran up an embankment on the other side! He said what unnerved him more than anything was how easily and quickly it got up that steep embankment. Sadly, I can't get any more details from Jimmy because he passed away not long ago from a heart condition that he contracted at an early age. He was a good man and will be sorely missed.

Not far from Pine Orchard, before you get into the town of Beatrice, is a little area called Kalem, with a population of about thirteen people. I received a phone call from a man in Florida who shared a lease with his father near here. The dad wouldn't talk to me, but the son did because he wanted some answers. It was early fall this past year, and they were in the middle of their property clearing out a small area to put up a ladder stand. As they were cutting limbs and small trees, they heard a loud yell. At first, they thought it must be the game warden, and they got quiet to see. The second yell was closer, and they realized this was no man, and it was not any animal they had ever heard before. It was very deep and very loud. Not long afterward, they started hearing the snapping of limbs, and it sounded like trees were being torn in half. They described it as sounding like a bulldozer! They decided it was smart to get out.

When they got back home, the son did some research and saw how close Evergreen was and read about the lore. He made a few phone calls, and someone gave him my number. I reassured him he wasn't crazy, and I never heard back from them. The dad still refuses to talk about it.

There have been multiple road-crossing stories that I haven't mentioned. One was near Castleberry, very close to Lennox and Range, and, of course, near Burnt Corn Creek. A man was traveling to work when a huge reddish-brown creature walked across the road. The man was badly shaken and to this day will not travel that road. Lee got that report, and it was a topic of great discussion on the morning show. He got a great look at that creature.

On the interstate, in the same area near where Burnt Corn Creek crosses under, a family traveling north on I-65 saw two of them standing beside the road. They had no idea of the lore in the area until they got back home and started doing some research. They also called Lee.

A preacher traveling south on I-65 actually saw one late at night walking beside the interstate as if it was hitchhiking! He said it was taller than a speed limit sign. He wasn't going to say a word about it, but his wife made him call the radio station because she was scared that one day someone was going to get hurt by this creature, and she wanted people to know that they are out there.

I talked with a forester a while back who works in the woods every day. He was in an area on the south end of Escambia County, not far from the Florida line. He said he would go into one particular spot every morning, drink his coffee, and plan his day. One morning, he was sipping his coffee when he was studying three large pine trees outside his window. Something seemed odd because, the day before, there were two trees, and now, in front of him, there were three. He was going through this in his mind when the third tree turned and walked away! He was floored and said it completely changed the way he looked at the woods. He said he will not ever go back into the woods without a gun, even though a gun isn't nearly big enough!

I talked with another forester who had a similar experience. He was traveling on the south end of Monroe County working a job when, in the middle of the day, a red, hairy creature walked out in front of him as he was traveling down the road. He told me specifically it was at eleven o'clock in the morning. The sun was out bright, and there was no doubt what he saw. He doesn't care if people believe him or not. There was no mistaking it.

My last story I will tell you is from an area that is a good piece from Monroeville and Evergreen, in a town called Marion. This place isn't very far from Selma. The Cahaba River runs through here, which flows into the Alabama River as it hits Selma. My friend Tommy had access to some old family property here, and it is absolutely one of the prettiest spots I have ever stepped on. It's a hundred-year-old ranch that rolls down to the Cahaba River. There is absolutely no access to this place whatsoever unless you're traveling by canoe. This is my kind of place!

I'm not going to lie; at least once a year, my old friends Tommy and Lavon and I, and whoever else was brave enough to travel, would go here and rough it out for a few days. We called it our man trip. It was basically fishing, swimming, four-wheeler riding, cooking, smoking cigars, and destroying our livers with alcohol for about three straight days! It was nonstop with very little sleep.

After we ate one night, Tommy got a big fire going in the backyard of the old run-down farmhouse. As we were huddled around the fire, we heard footsteps approaching an old catch pen that was about seventy-five yards away. We thought nothing of it until suddenly we heard a loud, ear-popping *whoop*! To this day, that is the only whoop I have ever heard, and it totally blew all of our minds. Every coyote within a hundred miles, it seemed, in every direction, went nuts for an hour! I have no idea what that call means, but it got the coyotes excited and really impressed us. All Lavon could mumble at that time of the night was, "That sure wasn't a coyote!" No, Lavon, it sure wasn't!

The next year, we came back, and during the day, we decided to tube on the Cahaba from one side of the property to the other. We were looking for arrowheads and artifacts. I had found several on the sandbars in this place. What a great way to relax and drink more beer! We parked our four-wheelers on a large bluff overlooking the river. We scaled down and swam to a sandbar on the other side. As we were looking for arrowheads and shark teeth, I noticed the sand was disturbed on the other end and walked toward it. I couldn't believe what I found. There were wet footprints walking out of the river and into the disturbance! When I examined the area, I saw it was a fresh parcel of mussels and clams that was in the process of being dug up. It looked like the creature ran across the sandbar and up a deer trail on the other side. Not one of us could jump from one track to the other, and they were fairly deep.

I believe we caught the creature digging up the mussels when our four-wheelers came to the bluff. Hearing the commotion, it quickly ran off. The tracks were about thirteen inches long, but they were very heavy. This was a very hard-packed gravel sandbar that was more like cement. Tommy was pushing three hundred pounds and couldn't leave a dent! These footprints were over three inches deep. We all saw it, but, of course, none of us had our phones to snap a picture because we were scared of getting them wet. My dad was with us that day, and Jeff, who is a good family friend and a big nonbeliever, but to this day he still has no answer for what we saw!

So, again, these are some of the stories. I have several more of hunters being run out of the woods and tons more road crossings. I love to collect them because they fascinate me, and I love looking at the similarities. We learn a lot that way. It also validates my experiences and helps me convince myself that I'm not all that crazy! I get asked all the time if I would shoot one. First, anyone who does such a thing who is not prepared, or not in fear for his life, could be asking for big trouble. According to the GCBRO, these things are rarely by themselves. I have told people on several occasions, "Don't fear the one that you see; you better fear the one that you don't see." These monsters have a history of attacking, and they will if they feel threatened or if you just happen to run across one that's a little territorial.

There are horror stories out there, I promise, and many people who have encountered them face-to-face said it was like looking at the devil himself. Pure evil and anger. I think, for the most part, through the years they have learned that humans are dangerous, and they stay away. But occasionally, one gets too close. I will not hesitate to defend myself, my family, or my livestock. Also, I will not hesitate to help anyone else who has the same issues. In the right circumstance, I will not hesitate to shoot the one in Pine Orchard! He owes me a good dog and some lost sleep!

We will never truly know if they exist or understand anything about them until we have a body—alive or dead. Then we can work toward understanding them and maybe protecting them, although they obviously do not need our protection. I cannot say with 100 percent certainty that these creatures exist. I have not seen one close-up, face-to-face, but have had tons of experience and stories that I cannot explain. Where there is smoke, there is usually a fire, and down here in Lower Alabama, there seems to be a lot of smoke!

But one thing is for sure: there is something out here in these swamps. Something that can't be explained. Something that people see and are terrified of. Something that defies all logic and will put your brain in a pure panic. So, if you're ever traveling down here in Lower Alabama and you happen to stop, and things get quiet, and the crickets stop chirping, and your hair starts to stand up on end, you might want to go ahead and get out of here! Or you may wind up with a story to add to the list!

Leah at Cooper's Bigfoot birthday party

Cooper helping me with research

My mother-in-law wrote me a poem for Christmas one year that sums it up pretty well. I think I will close with it! God bless!

There is an Ancient Legend told of a
Mysterious Bigfoot Beast.
Not just local Lore but from around the Globe.

The Yeti, Sasquatch, and Bigfoot.
Some have heard His Footsteps,
Other heard His Scream.
A Few Claim a Glimpse at His
Dark Shadowy Form.
But rarely is He ever seen.

His Scream brings Chills,
His Footsteps bring Fright.
To most just pure Terror!

But for some of Us these things bring
A Yearning to Search, hoping for
The Elusive Proof ... just the Truth.

Real or Legend you ask ...

All I can tell you is that once you have
Heard or Seen ... Then and Only Then ...
Will you Believe in the
Mysterious Bigfoot Beast ...

—B. Wiggins

REFERENCES

Allen, Jae. "How to Measure a Bear's Weight from Its Foot Size." *Sciencing.* April 29, 2018. Retrieved June 19, 2021, from https://sciencing.com/measure-bears-weight-its-foot-size-10069146.html.

Blackburn, Lyle. *Beyond Boggy Creek: In Search of the Southern Sasquatch.* Anomalist Books, 2017.

Crabtree, J. E. *Smokey and the Fouke Monster.* Days Creek Production Corporation, 1974.

Davis, M. K. "About M. K. Davis." The Davis Report. Unknown date. Retrieved November 10, 2020, from https://thedavisreport.wordpress.com/about/.

Harris, Tom. "How Bigfoot Works." How Stuff Works. Unknown date. Retrieved June 19, 2021, from https://science.howstuffworks.com/science-vs-myth/strange-creatures/bigfoot.htm/printable.

Marris, Emma. "How Primates Crossed Continents." *Nature.* March 3, 2008. Retrieved from https://www.nature.com/articles/news.2008.637.

McGhaw, Kaiya. "American Black Bear." *Encyclopedia of Alabama.* February 3, 2019. Retrieved June 19, 2021, from www.encyclopediaofalabama.org/article/h-4068?printable=true.

Strauss, Mark. "The Largest Ape That Ever Lived Was Doomed By Its Size." *National Geographic.* January 5, 2016. Retrieved from https://www.nationalgeographic.com/science/article/160106-science-evolution-apes-giant.

The Legend of Boggy Creek. Charles Pierce. Howco International Pictures, 1972.

Toole, Daniel. "Black Bears." *Outdoor Alabama.* Unknown date. Retrieved June 19, 2021, from https://www.outdooralabama.com/carnivores/black-bear.

Printed in the United States
by Baker & Taylor Publisher Services